MYCENAE

AGAMEMNON'S CAPITAL

The Site in its Setting

For all those whose help and company I have enjoyed at Mycenae

MYCENAE

AGAMEMNON'S CAPITAL

The Site in its Setting

Elizabeth French

TEMPUS

First published 2002

PUBLISHED IN THE UNITED KINGDOM BY:
Tempus Publishing Ltd
The Mill, Brimscombe Port
Stroud, Gloucestershire GL5 2QG
www.tempus-publishing.com

PUBLISHED IN THE UNITED STATES OF AMERICA BY:
Tempus Publishing Inc.
2A Cumberland Street
Charleston, SC 29401
www.tempuspublishing.com

British Library Cataloguing in Publication Data.
A catalogue record for this book is available from the British Library.

ISBN 0 7524 1951 X

Typesetting and origination by Tempus Publishing.
PRINTED AND BOUND IN GREAT BRITAIN.

Contents

List of illustrations

Text figures

Colour plates

Introduction

It is now over 60 years since I first saw Mycenae. I was 'actively present' at the excavations of 1939 and have taken part in all subsequent excavations by the British on the site with the exception of 1964, first as trench supervisor at the Cyclopean Terrace Building, the House of Sphinxes and the South House Annex, and then as pottery supervisor, conservator, assistant photographer and general factotum for the last three seasons on the Citadel House Area. Since 1970 we have spent almost every summer first in Nauplion and most recently in Mycenae itself working on the finds for publication and this work continues. With Ken Wardle, I edit the series of fascicules, under the title *Well Built Mycenae*, which cover the Citadel House Area excavation. This excavation like that of Grave Circle B was particularly important as it gave a unique opportunity to investigate and clarify points which earlier excavation of similar structures had left unclear. The Citadel House Area was the last untouched area within the citadel and the results obtained have allowed reanalysis of much of the work of Schliemann and Tsountas on the acropolis. The account that follows is the first attempt to set down this reconsideration in what I hope is a comprehensible way.

A short primary bibliography is given. References for everything outside the citadel will be found in French & Iakovides forthcoming and inside the citadel in Iakovides 1983. For the benefit of those writing essays, key general and specific works are also listed. For the few really controversial topics I have given special references. These are mainly to allow colleagues to find the evidence which I have used – there is nothing more annoying that not being able to chase up a doubtful point. I have tried to make it clear when something is merely my opinion but there are many occasions when I cannot now trace the logic behind my own ideas. The whole book has been discussed in detail with Kim Shelton and owes a very great deal to her willingness to consider outrageous ideas on my behalf. She is not, however, responsible for the result though I believe she largely agrees with it. The ideas of others too have been widely canvassed, particularly Ken and Diana Wardle on everything, Imma Kilian-Dirlmeir on the shaft graves, the Vaphio tomb and much else, Joseph Maran on palaces of all periods in the Argolid, John Killen on Linear B, Jacke Phillips on all things Egyptian, and Gunnel Ekroth on later Mycenae. Others, like Sir John Boardman, have kindly answered specific queries. I have unashamedly raided work in progress both by the contributors to *Well Built Mycenae* and by several PhD students who have consulted me. To the questions of students and especially from the young archaeologists who are working so tirelessly on the new museum at Mycenae, I owe my knowledge of the problems and what has not previously been made clear. Many of the drawings, though based on previous work, have been specially drawn

DATE	PERIOD & External Events	MAJOR EVENTS AT MYCENAE	Correlations
2000 +/-	Middle Helladic Starts		
		[Palace I]	
1675-1550		Grave Circle B	
1610-1490		Grave Circle A	D=after 1577 E
1600	Late Helladic Starts: EARLY PALATIAL		
1525 +/-	Eruption of Thera		
1525-1450	LH IIA	Early Tholos and Chamber Tombs	E
		[Palace II]	
1450-1410	LH IIB	[Palace III]	
1410-1370	LH IIIA1 : PALATIAL		
		Treasury of Atreus Built	
1370-1300	LH IIIA2		
	Mycenaean Pottery at Tell el Amarna		E
		First Fortification Wall	
		Palace IV	
	Ulu Burun Wreck		D=after 1305 E
		Tomb of Clytemnestra Built	
1300-1230	LH IIIB1	Extensive Settlement Building	
		West Extension of Fortification Wall	
1230		DISASTER ? Earthquake	
1230-1210	LH IIIB2	Palace V	
1210 1175	LH IIIB/C	Northeast Extension of Fortification Wall	
1200		DESTRUCTION largely with burning	
	POSTPALATIAL		
1175	LH IIIC	Rebuilding in some areas	
		? Palace VI	
1125		Khania burial platform	
1075		Destruction with burning	

1 *Chronological Chart. The letters in the right-hand column indicate correlations with dendrochronological (D) and with Egyptian dating (E)*

by Sibby Postgate to incorporate new suggestions. For publication photographs mainly originating in the Mycenae Archive I owe a great debt to the skills of Graham Norrie of the Department of Ancient History and Archaeology at Birmingham. I have attempted to name the actual source of all illustrations but some few have had to remain unassigned.

The glossary is included at the request of a friend who has picked out for me the words to be included. I am sorry if we have missed some terms which are puzzling. The index is computer generated but I have tried to edit it to be a useful tool rather than a completely exhaustive list.

I have stuck to more or less conventional period names not only because they are what come automatically to my mind but because they are those that will be found on museum labels, both in Greece and elsewhere (e.g. the British Museum). The actual chronology too is conventional – somewhat to my own surprise. I am as well aware as anyone today that bristle-cone pines and ice cores seem to indicate the need for an upward revision of the date for the eruption of Thera which destroyed the site of Akrotiri – contemporary with Grave Circle A. However the evidence from Egypt presented at the Mycenaean Seminar in London in 1998 by Jacke Phillips made it clear that this will not fit the Egyptian correlations, many of which are fixed by absolute lengths of reign in regnal years. This remains true (and has been rechecked August 2001) despite recent publications. Thus the chart (**1**) gives an outline of what we know for certain at the moment. Alas the latest dendrochronological work on material from Mycenae itself does not give much help, though I thank Peter Kuniholme and his assistants most warmly for answering my queries.

Many of the illustrations include scales in m/cm as is usual in Aegean archaeology. A 2m ranging rod stands 6ft 6in high; a 10cm scale measures just under 4in. Where no scale is reproduced a measurement in both systems is given in the caption.

1 The physical setting

The citadel of Mycenae (**colour plate 1**) occupies a rocky knoll which nestles between two of the higher (but not the highest) peaks of the Arachneion range of the north-east Peloponnese. The history of the site is closely linked to its position and thus a summary of its geophysical setting must form a basic introduction.

The plain of Argos

The plain forms the central feature of the north-east Peloponnese. The Peloponnese was itself described by Strabo as the leaf of a plane tree. It had reached its present shape by about 10,000 BC and conditions in the Late Bronze Age would have been very similar to those of some 50 years ago. The plain of Argos (**2 & 3**) lies at the head of an extensive gulf. The plain is bounded on the west by the Artemision range which extends southward down the coast as the Parnon range. On the east the Arachneion range continues southward with barren hills along the Argive peninsula. All these ranges of the east Peloponnese are basically of limestone with the exception of the hills at the south-east end of the peninsula which are of sandstone and the volcanic area of Methana. There is arable land in the lowlands of the plain and also in the high plateaux of the surrounding hills. The hills offer grazing as well as supplies of wood. A few of the mountains extend above the tree line. Recent work suggests that the major change in the physical aspects of the Argolid occurred during the Early Bronze Age (the third millennium BC) when badly managed land exploitation caused considerable erosion. However the effect was less obvious on the east and north of the plain, and it may be that little changed until the modern introduction of the tractor and of citrus trees brought about the drastic lowering of the water-table that now dominates agriculture throughout the plain. Certainly there would have been heavy fluctuations in rainfall but no more than recently and rainfall may have been more regular in the valleys surrounded by hills to the north-east. Water supply/moisture will always have been a crucial factor in the environment. It is clear from the precautions taken against flash flood that it was a well-known hazard, as too was earthquake. It has been suggested that it was in the Early Bronze Age also that the so-called Mediterranean triad in agriculture was introduced: cultivation of the olive, often with wheat or another cereal beneath the trees, and of the grape.

These features would have given the environment the visual aspect so often associated with Greece (**colour plates 3 & 4**) but now largely lost: a plain dotted with olive trees and hillsides with the typical shrubs of a garigue. Mycenae itself lies some eight miles (13km) from the sea at Tiryns which may well have been the port for the

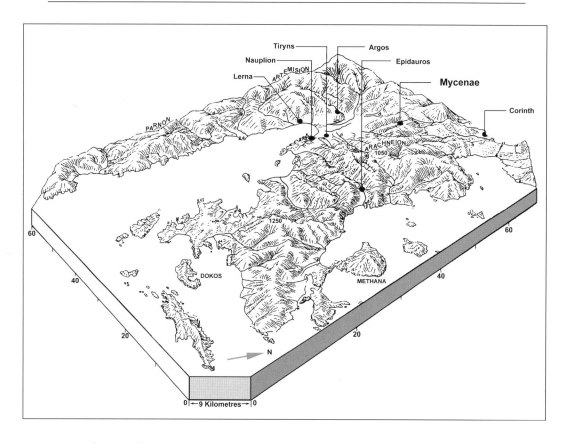

2   *North-east Peloponnese: the Gulf of Argos and the Argive Peninsula (Scale 9km =
5.58 miles).* After the *Admiralty Handbook* 1944, fig. 28

eastern half of the plain. The sea was nearer the actual site of Tiryns in antiquity and
the shelving beach would have served for ancient shipping. Though the routes
leading from Mycenae to the north are known, heavy cultivation has obliterated all
traces in the plain itself and a route leading on from the Argive Heraion to Tiryns
can only be conjectured. The major Mycenaean sites of the Argolid are shown in **3**
as well as the road system which linked them.

The site itself

The site lies tucked into the hills with a deep gorge (the Chavos) on the south and
another almost as precipitous (the Kokoretsa) on the north (**colour plates 1 & 5**),
suiting the Homeric description (*Odyssey* III, 263): 'in a corner of horse-rearing
Argos'. It commands a view to the south-west down the plain towards Argos (**colour
plate 6**) but there is no view from the citadel down the east side of the plain. Tiryns
and Midea cannot be seen from any part of the site and Nauplion only from the south

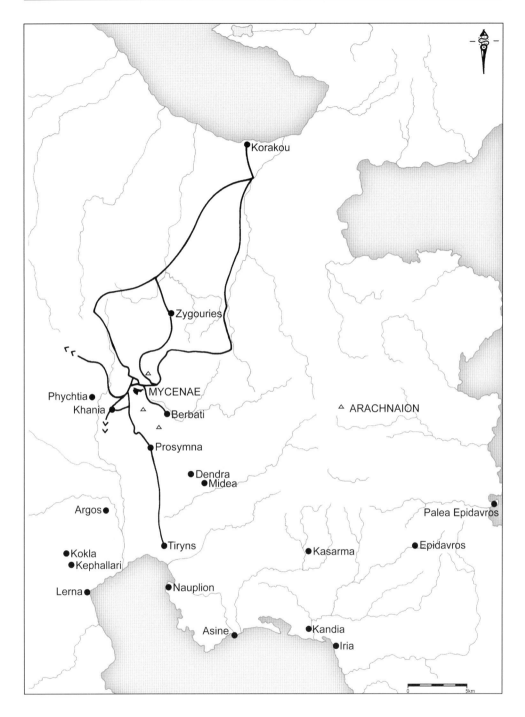

3 *North-east Peloponnese: the main Late Bronze Age sites and the road system radiating from Mycenae.* © Mycenae Archive

end of the Panagia ridge. Argos itself was clearly the communications centre for the plain and was undoubtedly the most important site during the first part of the second millennium. It was at the expense of Argos that Mycenae became the focal point of the plain – a situation resented by Argos in historical times and eventually redressed by her. Mycenae's position lay on the divide between arable and pasture land and afforded good lines of communication in all directions. A perpetual water supply was provided by the spring which we know as the Perseia in the pass to the east.

Though the view from the site is not extensive that from the watch point on the summit of Agios Elias which dominates the citadel is overwhelming and it is an easy ascent rather than a climb to reach the top. From here the description of the signal stations bringing the news of the capture of Troy that features at the beginning of Aeschylus' *Agamemnon* is entirely plausible. A series of heights running from Troy via Mt Ida, Lemnos, Mt Athos, on to Cithairon, and finally to Agios Elias of the Arachneion range are intervisible by day and certainly with beacons. This watch point combined with another on the Larissa at Argos would have given easy control over a wide area.

2 The background

Foundation and other legends

It is a measure of the importance of Mycenae that it features so extensively in legend. Long after the site had shrunk to a tiny settlement with little importance beyond a temple, its name was well known and the action of sending troops to fight the Persians was quite sufficient to annoy the more typically powerful Argos. In the *Iliad* and *Odyssey* the emphasis given to Mycenae is unique.

In legends referring to earlier periods, however, the whole Argolid seems to have been an area of smaller interrelated states – a situation not incompatible with the archaeological evidence. The legend suggests that Perseus after inadvertently fulfilling the prophecy of killing his grandfather Acrisius, king of Argos, exchanged the kingdom of Argos for that of Tiryns and then founded a new city for himself. Pausanias (II,15,4) tells us firmly 'it is known to the Greeks that Perseus founded Mycenae'. At least three sources for the name Mycenae are given: from Perseus' sword pommel 'mukos' (mushroom from its shape) which he dropped there; or from an actual mushroom which he picked to use as a cup when he was thirsty. Homer however in the Odyssey seems to derive the name from Mycene, a nymph of great beauty but of origins which vary from source to source.

To fortify his new city Perseus employed the Cyclops to build the walls and it is from this that this style of 'gigantic' masonry is named Cyclopean. The accounts of the royal succession of the Perseid dynasty are complex but eventually the family gives way to the Pelopids: Atreus and Thyestes and their descendants.

In the *Iliad* Agamemnon is portrayed as the leader of a confederacy, leading by force of his own character and because of his resources. He supplied 100 ships of his own and also gave inland Arcadia their contingent of another 60; he may also have supplied others of the more distant participants. The bounds of the kingdom as given in the 'Catalogue of Ships' extend north from the site of Mycenae itself and encompass part of the south coast of the Gulf of Corinth. It is Argos with Tiryns who controls the gulf of Argos and the Argolid peninsula. This division is not incompatible with the archaeological evidence, particularly the road network, for the thirteenth century BC. The inner circle of leaders numbers six, in addition to Agamemnon himself and Menelaus, his brother, husband of Helen and ruler of Lacedaimon (Sparta). Of the others, Nestor has pride of place for his seniority but his kingdom of Pylos which supplied 90 ships is now known to have been one of the important centres of the Peloponnese, if rather conservative in cultural terms. Ajax the Greater from Salamis is renowned for his physical prowess and Odysseus from Kephallenia and Ithaca for his cunning; neither brings a large contingent (12 ships each) but both areas are now recognised as established Mycenaean centres. Diomedes of Argos and Tiryns brings 80 ships as does Idomeneus of Crete. His inclusion in this group is of particular interest in assessing the interrelations of Crete and the mainland of Greece in the Late Bronze Age and the Early Iron Age. In central Greece, however, the inclusion of Ajax the Less from Locris, the exclusion of a ruler from Boeotia or Orchomenos from the inner circle of leaders and the puzzling reference to 'Lower Thebes' give rise to discussion. Recent archaeological discoveries are indeed revealing more important sites in Locris and its position on the gulf facing Euboea was important for shipping at that time. The lack of emphasis on Thebes can be interpreted as a reflection of the mythical destruction of the city which antedated the Trojan War. Archaeologically there are several substantial sites of the Late Bronze Age in the area but Thebes itself was also flourishing. It has now produced an archive of Linear B tablets and is being considered along with Mycenae itself as a potential candidate for the capital of Ahhiyawa as mentioned in Hittite records.

One anomaly of the Homeric situation is the offer to Achilles by Agamemnon of seven cities on the gulf in Messenia. We have no source for why these cities, which can be identified and are possible Late Bronze Age sites, should have been in the gift of the ruler of Mycenae.

It is the myths of Atreus and Thyestes and their children which form the subject of so many classical dramas and from them have influenced more recent dramatists such as O'Neill (*Mourning Becomes Electra*) and Eliot (*Family Reunion*). By the time of Aeschylus the city of Agamemnon is referred to as Argos – until recently a much more suitable setting for modern versions like Satre's *Les Mouches* – but the actual site descriptions in the *Agamemnon* are in fact based on the site of Mycenae and not Argos.

In recent times new legends have become prevalent. Copious and extraordinary treasures are reported to have been found when the Treasury of Atreus and the Tomb of Clyemnestra were opened in the nineteenth century. Moreover every modern inhabitant of the Argolid is sure that the Golden Chariot of Agamemnon is buried somewhere on the site and will ultimately be discovered.

History of discovery and excavation

The account of the site by Pausanias, the second-century AD Roman traveller, became available in translation in Western Europe in the late eighteenth century and was used as a guide book by many of the well-known nineteenth-century travellers. But before we reach them there are some puzzling anomalies to consider which are still under research. First is how the site was positioned on maps. It is correctly mentioned and placed in the *Tabula Peutingeriana* – the map/itinerary drawn up in the fourth century AD but based on earlier sources and ultimately on the Roman road system – which showed the routes of the whole Roman world. But, probably through copyists' errors, the grid references in the work of the second century AD Alexandrian geographer Ptolemy, which are astronomically based, are incorrect; thus when the early true cartographers made use of his work after it was first published at the end of the fifteenth century AD, Mycenae was placed to the south-west of Argos. It would seem that it was not until the 1680s that the site was correctly placed on general maps.

Secondly, confusion seems to have arisen through the misidentification of the site by the traveller Cyriac of Ancona in the early fifteenth century. It has been suggested by German scholars that he thought the fort at Katsingri (Agios Adrianos) east of Tiryns was the site of Mycenae. Traces of this misidentification seem to persist as Mycenae though correctly placed on a map of de Wit dated 1680 is labelled 'Charia Cast(ello?). Ag. Adrianos Mycenae'.

Thus we cannot be sure that any of the travellers of the late sixteenth and early seventeenth century actually visited the site but we have two clear mentions by French travellers in the mid-seventeenth century. Neither, however, refers to the Lion Gate though one speaks of an 'amphitheatre' (the Hellenistic theatre over the Tomb of Clytemnestra). The first account of the Lion Gate since Pausanias dates to 1700 when it is described by Francesco Vandeyk, an engineer in the service of the Venetians under Morrisoni. Vandeyk was particularly interested in the site as a potential source of good cut stone for building the new fortifications planned in Nauplion after the Venetian reconquest. It has been suggested in fact that the Lion Gate may well have been covered by debris and the famous relief not visible until cleared by Vandeyk. We can see the various stages by which the gateway was gradually fully cleared in a succession of drawings made during the early nineteenth century.

The first of the many illustrations of the site were made by another Frenchman, Michel Fourmont, who visited with his nephew in 1729 while supposedly making acquisitions for the French royal collections. His drawings are unprepossessing but his sketch map of the Argolid is a useful document. Several other maps of the area were made by the French during the century following this, culminating in the work published as *Expedition de la Moree* in 1834.

Fourmont's map unfortunately does not help to solve another problem: *when* the village moved from just south of the modern car park (traces can still be seen) where it was described by Vandeyk, to its present site where it is placed by Gell who visited in 1804-5.

The second half of the eighteenth century saw the expansion of the study and exploration of the remains of classical Greece. This was frustrated but in a way also made more interesting by the impediments to travel resulting from the French Revolution and the Napoleonic wars. Moreover the scholarly interests of the French excited both rivalry and fears that the interest was more military than scholarly.

In the first half of the nineteenth century Mycenae was visited by many. Lord Elgin and Lord Sligo were assisted by the Turkish governors to remove sculpted blocks from the Treasury of Atreus. The account by Lady Elgin (in a letter to her mother) of climbing into the tomb through the relieving triangle with the Governor's young son (who lost his hat) is remarkably vivid. We have important accounts of the site from Gell, Dodwell, Leake and others; most of these are accompanied by illustrations. Five of the nine tholos tombs were then known but not necessarily correctly identified as tombs (the Kato Phournos was thought to be a city gate); the other four had to wait for discovery until the end of the century.

The first investigative exploration seems to have been by Cockerell who cleared and had recorded the apex of the Treasury of Atreus. Gell, though he did not actually do any, advocated excavation at the site. Then, with the liberation of Greece from the Turks, the work of the Greek authorities begins: Kyriakos Pittakes carried out the final clearance of the Lion Gate approach in 1841. The whole period is marked by a stream of visitors, using maps and itineraries like those of Gell. Their accounts are scholarly and add little to our knowledge of the site. Their illustrations, however, can be very evocative. The charming watercolour by Edward Lear (**colour plate 2**) shows the site from the Panagia ridge silhouetted against the mountain behind with his usual scatter of a few shepherds.

By the time that Heinrich Schliemann began his work there was, unlike at Troy, no question about the identification of the site. He had visited the site in 1868 and began negotiating for a permit in 1870 but his actions at Troy caused problems. In frustration at the delays and difficulties, in February 1874 he sank 34 shafts in different places throughout the area before being stopped by the authorities. Despite this, full excavation began on 7 August 1876 in the area just within the Lion Gate where his test trenches had been particularly productive. Within a few weeks he had made the startling discoveries for which he has become known. He published a full account of the work within two years and it remains an amazing document – well worth reading. Of particular interest to archaeologists are his very perceptive stratigraphic comments as well as his highly up-to-date use of photography as the basis of the many engravings with which the book is illustrated. The introduction to the book was written by Gladstone – a striking testament to the importance of Homeric studies in the United Kingdom in the last half of the nineteenth century.

The permit which had been granted to Schliemann by the Greek authorities had conditions and it fell to Panaiotis Stamatakis to represent the Archaeological Society of Athens at the site and to try, rather vainly, to control Schliemann's exuberance. He also continued work after Schliemann's departure in 1877 and found the sixth shaft grave of Grave Circle A and with Vasilios Drosinos (Schliemann's surveyor) the so-called Acropolis Treasure – probably the contents of a looted shaft grave.

Among other contemporary sources one may be mentioned. William Simpson of the *Illustrated London News* visited in 1877 and published a detailed illustrated account of Schliemann's work. Simpson lived in the village in the house of one of the Christopoulos family where, he tells us, the Schliemanns too had lodged. Unfortunately, as we realise from study of Simpson's illustration, this house is no longer standing.

For the archaeologists who were to follow, perhaps the most important development of this period of research were the maps prepared by the German military engineer, Bernard Steffen. In the course of the cold and snowy winter of 1881-2 – at the instigation of Curtius of the German Archaeological Institute in Athens – he surveyed and published maps both of the Acropolis of Mycenae (with an inset of

Tiryns) and the territory surrounding the site. These remained the only full surveys for a hundred years. They record, with formidable accuracy, the site immediately after it was left by Schliemann and before the work of Christos Tsountas. The evidence they contain is quite without parallel.

Shortly after this the work of Tsountas begins. He worked on the site from 1884 to 1902, though excavating also in Thessaly during this period. It is to Tsountas that we owe the almost total clearance of the acropolis (including the Palace) and the excavation of over 100 chamber tombs and a further four tholos tombs. In 1893 he published first in Greek and then in English (with J.L. Manatt) a book presenting his finds to date, *Mycenaean Age*. He was a brilliant scholar and his interpretations are always both lucid and penetrating. Unfortunately however he did not keep the full range of his finds (particular pot sherds) nor did he publish fully. It is further unfortunate that four of his notebooks are missing.

With the turn of the century attention moved to Knossos in Crete where Arthur Evans' new discoveries were rivalling those of Schliemann. Though minor work was carried out at Mycenae by several scholars, it was not until 1920, when the First World War was over and excavation at Knossos had become more routine, that Evans himself suggested that the British School at Athens should undertake research at Mycenae. Professor Tsountas agreed to allow my father, Alan Wace (whose work was well known to him from his excavations in Thessaly), to excavate on the site. There then began a series of excavations that were to continue, off and on, until Wace's death in 1957 and indeed beyond.

The first period of work under Wace's direction took place between 1920 and 1923. The primary work comprised detailed study and restudy of many of the areas excavated by Schliemann and Tsountas, notably the Lion Gate, the Granary, the Grave Circle, the Palace and the tholos tombs. But a particularly important section deals with Hellenistic Mycenae, thanks to a crucial inscription newly found. A further 24 chamber tombs were carefully excavated partly in a cemetery (on the Kalkani hill) which had not been previously explored. Their full publication still accounts for half the published tomb reports from the site. The second period of excavation consisted of only a single year in 1939 cut off by the outbreak of the Second World War. This season concentrated on problems that had arisen in the intervening period: the date of the Treasury of Atreus (which had been challenged by Evans), the Prehistoric Cemetery (originally an idea of Tsountas'), the Archaic temple and its surroundings on the summit of the acropolis, and various other areas like the House of Columns and the chance find of Lisa's House by the Epano Phournos tomb, where less extensive exploration was carried out. Much of this material was published in general terms in Wace 1949 though final study of some sections, notably the Prehistoric Cemetery and the Archaic temple, has only recently been completed. The third period of work by Wace took place between 1950 and 1955 (when a moratorium on excavation on the site was imposed by the Greek authorities). Time was spent on the completion of the various projects started in 1939 but the most notable work was the excavation of the group of 'houses' now fully published as the Ivory Houses. These lay south of the Tomb of Clytemnestra and proved to be both diverse and richly endowed. The most pleasing find was that of tablets in the Linear B script in well-documented contexts (**58** left was the first). After Wace's death in 1957, permission was sought to complete work on the area within the fortification walls between the South House and Tsountas' House – the only untouched area within the walls – which had been started in 1954. Lord William Taylour was in charge of this excavation, on what became known as the Citadel House Area, with the more active co-operation of the Archaeological Society of Athens (whose concession the site had always been) but we had little idea what would be involved. The excavation itself proved a long and difficult one, covering a further seven seasons of work and has been followed to date by over 30 years of study. During the excavation the Archaeological Society was represented first by Dr Ioannis Papadimitriou and later by Professor George Mylonas. The soil held up by the fortification wall was extremely deep, reaching some 16m in places. The stratigraphy revealed, as we excavated, an important section of the Hellenistic town, graves of the Early Iron Age, deep levels, mainly wash, of the late Post-Palatial period, an important set of structures of the first Post-Palatial period, a complex of buildings of the Palatial period which Professor Mylonas rightly recognised as part of a multi-faceted Cult Centre – these had been protected from depredation by the deep soil levels covering them and contained unique cultic equipment – and in the lowest levels above the rock more graves of the Prehistoric Cemetery and traces of early Neolithic habitation of the site. This work is in course of publication. It has been largely funded by the Mediterranean Archaeological Trust supplemented by grants from the Institute for Aegean Prehistory and by generous donations from some of those who enjoyed working on the site under my father.

Various preservation and conservation projects had been carried out over the years (notably to the Tomb of Clytemnestra) but it was between 1950 and 1957 that the Greek Government Service for the Preservation and Restoration of Ancient Monuments (known briefly as the Anastylosis) undertook a vast programme of work at the site. The fortification walls in particular were widely restored (including lifting the two blocks back beside the Lion Gate relief), the corner of the megaron of the Palace rebuilt and the damage to the dome of the Tomb of Clytemnestra repaired. It was during this project that in late 1951 the workmen came upon the first grave – Alpha – of Grave Circle B. It was immediately realised that this was a unique find and its excavation was entrusted to a group of the leading prehistorians of the day: Dr Ioannis Papadimitriou, at that time in charge of work in the Argolid, Professor Antonios Keramopoulos, the veteran excavator of Thebes, Professor Spiridon Marinatos of the University of Athens, and Professor George Mylonas of Washington University, St Louis, Missouri. This work continued until 1955 and was subsequently published by Mylonas (following the death of Papadimitriou in 1963).

The interest in the site excited first by the restorations and secondly by the new grave circle led to further excavation from 1958 onwards by the Archaeological Society under the direction of Professor Mylonas assisted by his daughter Ione Mylonas Shear (the Panagia Houses) and Professor T. Lesie Shear Jnr (the Enyalios sanctuary and work on the citadel). Professor Spiros Iakovides worked with Professor

Mylonas from 1984 and continued the excavation alone after Mylonas' death from 1987 until 1989 when lack of storage space forced a moratorium. This material has been given preliminary publication in the Praktika of the Archaeological Society and is currently under detailed study.

From 1991 to 1994 the British School under my direction undertook a survey project at Mycenae in co-operation with Professor Iakovides for the Archaeological Society. The aim was to record accurately the position of all test excavations and ancient remains (particularly the mass of chamber tombs) that could be identified outside the walls and to check all the antiquities which had been recorded by Steffen on his map: did they still exist and to what date could they now be assigned? Subsequently a new modern plan of the citadel was completed by a team of surveyors from the technical university. All this work, with chapters on every aspect of the site, is being published by the Archaeological Society under the title *Mycenae Atlas*. In the course of the work we all learnt a great deal about the site as a whole which it has been possible to incorporate into the text of this book.

Under the antiquities regulations of Greece, chance finds and emergency work fall generally under the officers of the Antiquities Service, though additional funding and thus also publication can on occasion be supplied by the Archaeological Society. Thus Dr Papadimitriou with his assistant Dr Petsas excavated widely in the early 1950s and later Dr Nicolas Verdelis cleared the West House, uncovered when the road to the citadel past the Ivory Houses was widened. He also cleared several chamber tombs. More recent work has been done by Zoe Aslamatizou (the Souleimani cemetery) and the late Dr Artemis Onasoglou (the site for the new Museum). Eleni Palaiologou, who has been in charge of the site for the Archaeological Service for some years, has excavated a very considerable number of tombs, many found when tracks to the fields were made suitable for tractor access. In 2000 a new period of excavation was initiated by Professor Iakovides who with his assistant, Dr Kim Shelton, returned to complete and extend excavation on Petsas' House in the Pezoulia area.

3 Early history

While it is not possible actually to describe Mycenae during the first millennia of her occupation we can perhaps suggest something of what the site must have been like on the basis of comparison with other sites where excavation and study of these periods has been possible. Though occupation earlier than the floruit of Mycenae in the Late Bronze Age has been known since the first major excavations – those of Schliemann in the 1870s – it is only with more recent work that the very earliest material has been identified.

Sherds of the early Neolithic period (of the so-called Rainbow Ware of which handsome examples were found at Nemea: Tsoungiza and are displayed in the Corinth Museum) were first found quite unexpectedly at the very end of the 1966 excavation season encased in extremely hard soil which at first had been thought to be rock. This stratum lay on the west side of the citadel under the Citadel House Area. Following this discovery the sherd evidence from all the deep levels of that area which was still under excavation and study was even more carefully scrutinised for early material. Current research is now concentrated on ascertaining, as far as this sherd evidence in secondary contexts allows, whether the site was continuously occupied from the seventh millennium and which areas of the site were occupied in which periods. Unfortunately little more evidence concerning these early periods is recoverable without environmental samples, house plans and small artifacts.

Mycenae would not necessarily have been a leading site in these periods. For instance, we assume that it was less important than Lerna in the Neolithic and Early Bronze Age and know that it was less important than Lerna and Argos in the earlier part of the Middle Bronze Age. Sites even less important have, however, been noted in the region of Mycenae. Early and Middle Helladic material has long been known from the top of the Kalkani hill to the west where a part of the Late Bronze Age cemetery was located. Survey has also identified a small Early Bronze Age site to the south at Monastiraki: Gourmades.

Neolithic sites in the Argolid are not prolific. They comprise both typical open mound sites like Lerna itself and a few other small sites in similar positions and large cave sites like the Kephalari Cave from where there is striking material of the middle and late Neolithic periods. (Material from Lerna is exhibited in Argos and that from the Kephalari Cave resembles that from the Francthi Cave exhibited in Nauplion.) In fact Neolithic settlement at Mycenae does not fit well into either of these models. The first are thought to be the basic communities of the first farmers who settled and built mud brick houses, who cultivated crops and exploited domesticated animals, notably sheep, and who mastered several important craft skills: wood, stone and bone

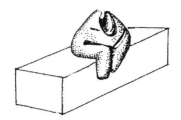

4 Seated female figurine of pale steatite, possibly of Neolithic date, which had been used as a pendant from a storeroom below the Megaron in the Cult Centre (62-1757 MM 11276; life-size).
© Mycenae Archive

working, pottery manufacture and eventually metalworking. It has been suggested that the caves may have played a role in sheep herding but the quantities of first-class pottery found in them would imply a more elaborate function. As well as sherd evidence Mycenae has produced one artifact which *may* have been produced in the Neolithic period (**4**): a tiny stone figurine was found in a store room of the Late Bronze Age. It had clearly been used for long periods as an amulet as the hole for the string had been enlarged and worn through by the string.

The evidence for the Early Bronze Age at Mycenae is more prevalent. Interestingly it occurs in the deep levels both on the top of the acropolis hill under the various areas of the Palace and at the west. Here in the area near the Great Ramp there was a considerable depth of Early Helladic wash representing all three phases of the period. We cannot identify the source of this wash. Early Helladic pottery is also very prevalent in the area outside the walls near and to the south-west of the Tomb of Aegisthus. The source of this material is not known but it may be a further extension of the wash levels found within the walls. From the foot of the Great Ramp came a restorable bowl of Early Helladic I style which might indicate the presence of a grave. Other probably grave pots were found by Stamatakis nearby but these date from Early Helladic III and are likely to mark the beginning of the major cemetery which covered the west slope of the hill in the Middle Bronze Age (**5**). There is nothing however to help us describe the settlement. At both Lerna and Tiryns large important buildings indicate special status either for some of the population or for the sites them-selves. The House of Tiles at Lerna was not only an important and well-built structure but it contained a group of sealings which show some form of administrative control. Lerna also is enclosed by a sturdy fortification wall. The round building at Tiryns is to date without parallel and is currently being re-excavated and restudied. Both these buildings stood at the highest point of their respective sites and the presence of so much Early Helladic pottery high on the Mycenae acropolis probably indicates some sort of similar structural symbol. Sites like Lerna and Tiryns are relatively extensive and elsewhere on the mainland there is clear evidence of town planning though, on the whole, not as sophisticated as on the Cycladic islands. A further group of sites founded at this period, of which several lie on or opposite the Argive peninsula, are situated on rocky knolls by the sea and can be linked to the maritime trade in obsidian from Melos (so common that it forms one of the type artifacts for the identification of Early Bronze Age sites in survey), in pottery which is documented by a wreck off the island of Dokos and presumably other more perishable products.

The Early Bronze Age had been thought to be the period when agriculture developed a wider base with the inclusion of the cultivation of the grape and the olive together with that of cereals – the so-called 'Mediterranean triad' – but this theory has been questioned and more evidence is needed. Almost no tombs of this period have been found in the Argolid but those from Zygouries (by Agios Basilios, just over the boundary into Corinthia) allow us to appreciate both the range of pottery and of small objects of this time (exhibited in Corinth).

4 The Pre-Palatial period

We know rather more about Mycenae in the Middle Bronze Age but here there is a different problem that must be confronted: the extreme difference in the cultural level, particularly the availability of wealth, between the beginning and the end of the period. Throughout the mainland of Greece the start of the Middle Bronze Age appears to see a regression in the evolution of 'civilization' (as defined by Renfrew in *The Emergence of Civilization*). Descriptions of these people, almost certainly newcomers to the area, vary between a polite 'well-defined difference in their cultural achievement' to the rude nickname of 'Grey Minyans' (after their distinctive pottery). This period, in fact, starts with the pottery phase Early Helladic III, which is distinct in many ways from what preceded it but shares features with the following phases. This material is found at Lerna particularly in levels immediately succeeding a heavy burning (which destroyed the House of Tiles). The period ends with the two Grave Circles A & B which will be described separately below.

Occupation of the Middle Helladic period at Mycenae is known both from scattered traces of walls and from the copious amounts of excellent pottery found in most later contexts. Obviously walls are only known where the lower levels, often encased in the heavy terraces used to support later buildings, have been excavated. On the top of the acropolis, walls thought to be Middle Helladic have been found below the Great Court and in the lower strata of the Pithos Area, and in a deposit on the north slope beyond the terrace of the later temple. These may once again indicate that there was a main residence or central building at the highest point of the site. Other remains have been found beyond the entrance of the House of Columns and of House Delta. On the west slope there are remains of this period in the area of Lion Gate, under the Ramp House and below the Citadel House Area. The most extensive structure yet known, however, was found beside the later Processional Way that links the Cult Centre at the west to the Palace. Here lay the burnt remains of a basement storeroom, filled with pots and provisions.

Outside the walls there are structural remains by Grave Circle B as well as near and under the Ivory Houses group. On the Panagia Ridge, though Middle Helladic sherds occurred in the area of the Treasury of Atreus, none were found as far south as the House of Lead at the far end of the upper section of the ridge. Another area of settlement lay on the Kalkani hill further to the west. As with the earlier periods current research is attempting, by studying all the stray material, to ascertain whether the occupation of the site was continuous and which areas were in use in which of the subphases of the period.

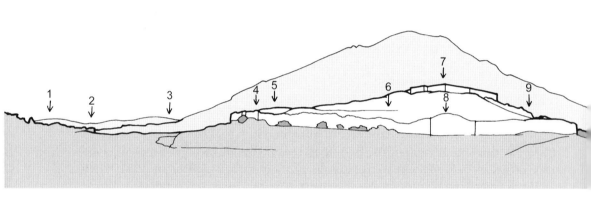

5   *View of the site from the south-west showing the extent of the Prehistoric Cemetery of*
    the Middle Bronze Age and the setting of other major features.
    © Mycenae Archive G.H. Norrie
    1. Grave Circle B
    2. Tomb of Clytemnestra with the Hellenistic Theatre over the dromos
    3. Tomb of Aegisthus marking the west end of the Prehistoric Cemetery
    4. Lion Gate
    5. Grave Circle A
    6. Cult Centre
    7. Palace
    8. Hellenistic Tower perhaps the site of the original West Gate
    9. South end of the Prehistoric Cemetery under the South-West Quarter

Much of the lower west slope of the acropolis hill (both inside and outside the later citadel wall) was covered by a large diffuse cemetery known as the Prehistoric Cemetery (**5**). The overall cemetery includes the two Grave Circles but in addition well over 100 small graves of individuals have been found wherever excavation has been able to reach the underlying rock. Many more must still lie covered by the latter structures. This cemetery was presumably external to the main settlement and those in outlying areas would have been interred near where they lived. To call it a cemetery may in fact be too precise; it may be that burials were made on the lower slopes of the hill, in areas not occupied by housing, without actual planning.

What is not clear is whether the apparent austerity which is shown in these simple tombs was reflected in the living conditions or not. There is quite clearly a change from the Early Bronze Age but the period may well not have been as poor and primitive as some scholars have suggested. The artifacts that we have are well made and show the introduction of several important new features. Pottery is for the first time almost exclusively wheelmade. The handsome Grey Minyan ware may well be an imitation of silver and metal prototypes are deliberately echoed in various ways: studs at the top of the handle where it joins the rim, ring handles, heavy carinations and ringed stems on goblets, beak spouts. It therefore seems most likely that there were ample metal vessels to be imitated and it is only because of the austerity of the actual graves that none have survived. A new type of decoration using manganese in the thin clay used as paint gives a matt effect which is exploited in various decorative schemes. These pottery wares are quite different from but just as competently produced as contemporary wares from Crete which were exported to Egypt and the Levant.

The increase in visible wealth and change in culture that is both so marked at Mycenae towards the end of the period and so intriguing can best be exemplified in Grave Circle B. This group of tombs was found by accident in 1951 when workmen were taking soil to cover the reconstructed cap of the dome of the Tomb of Clytemnestra. They came upon a stele, set in a base (**7**), and below it a shaft grave. (By definition a shaft grave is a large deep rectangular pit in the bottom of which a grave is placed; the distinguishing features are the depth and the presence of low rubble walls to support a roof over the grave.) The newly discovered group, which lies on a slight rise in the rock to the west of the main extent of the Prehistoric Cemetery, was surrounded by a wall which has been dated to the Middle Helladic period. Within the wall lay 25 graves (containing 35 individuals) of which 14 were shaft graves. There was also one larger built tomb (Rho) which is discussed below (p.47). They are known by the letters of the Greek alphabet to distinguish them from the graves found by Schliemann in Grave Circle A (as it now had to be called) which are known by Roman numerals. The earliest tombs are the simple cist graves and these can be dated to the end of Middle Helladic. The shaft graves belong to the last phase, just before the change to Late Helladic I in pottery terms, a transition marked by the introduction of pots with decoration in lustrous black on a pale ground – the beginning of true Mycenaean ware (**13**). A few burials are datable to LH I itself.

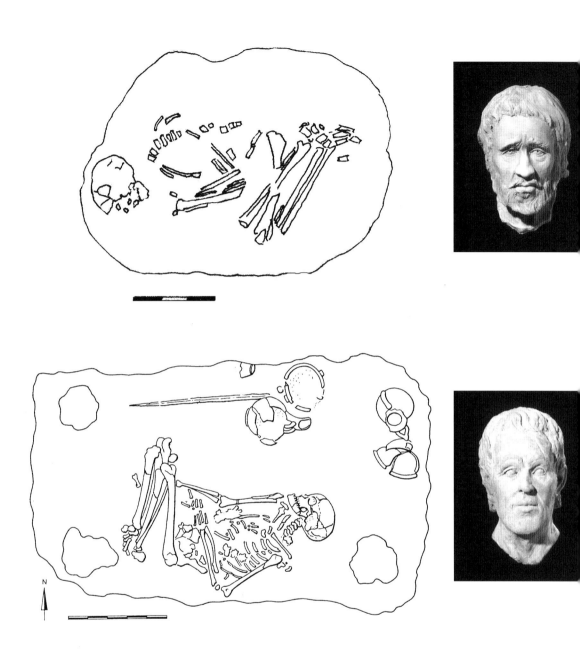

6   *(above and right) Graves Sigma, Zeta and Gamma of Grave Circle B to show the
growing elaboration of the graves and the reconstructed heads of those buried there.*
© University of Manchester

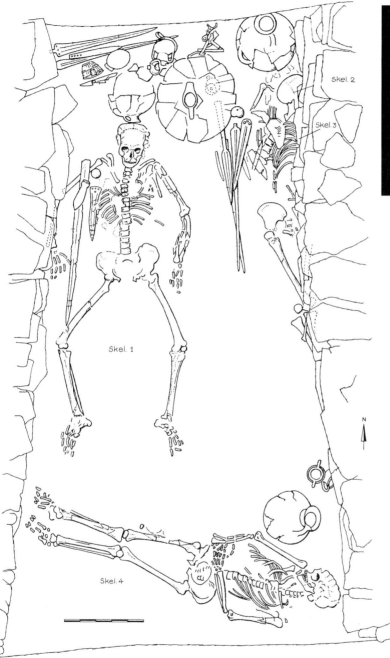

Skel. 2

Skel. 3

Skel. 1

Skel. 4

N

The facial reconstruction team at Manchester has produced seven heads, six men and one woman, in an attempt to seek family relationships among the population (Musgrave *et al.* 1995). Further research on this subject using DNA has also been carried out. These people will serve well to represent the development in the Grave Circle both of the people interred and the grave goods that accompanied them (**6**).

The most striking is Sigma 131, known affectionately as Pelops (**6**). His grave lay by itself on the south-east side of the circle and was marked by a heap of stones. It was a simple but deep cist grave of the type known from the Prehistoric Cemetery and contained one burial in a contracted position facing north with his head to the east. The skeleton, which was in good condition, shows that this was, as Professor Angel reports, 'a massively built man, quite tall with slight arthritis of the vertebrae'. Professor Angel had noted during the actual excavation some red-brown stones in the area of the lower ribs and identified these as gall-stones. Surprisingly he had only three diseased teeth in spite of an estimated age of about 55. There were no grave goods but the burial is assigned to the Middle Helladic period from sherds of Yellow and Grey Minyan ware and matt painted ware found in the deposit. It is possible that the scattered human bones also found in the deposit indicate earlier burials in this cist which were cleared out for a final interment.

Grave Zeta (**6**) is one of the first graves to show real changes both in the grave type and the presence of grave goods though the actual burial is still contracted and lying on its right side. The grave lies in the north-west quadrant of the circle and was marked by a row of stones indicating the perimeter. The cist itself is larger than the skeleton and quite deep; it has the holes for four posts in the corners to hold up a the roof which also rested on a wide cut ledge in the rock some 10in (25cm) below the top of the cutting. The skeleton, Z 59, was of another large man, aged about 49, resting on a pebbled floor. Angel describes him as 'very tall and broad shouldered with thick bones'. He too suffered from arthritis and had at least one badly decayed tooth. His skull was marked by depressions 'apparently results of heavy blows or wounds inflicted by a right-handed opponent'. He also had healed fractures of the spine and one of the ribs. In front of him in the grave was a simple undecorated long sword with ivory pommel as well as six vases: two Yellow Minyan goblets with deep bowls but traces of ribbing on the short stems, in matt painted ware a beaked jug, a straight-sided cup and a two handled cup of the type called a 'kantharos' and finally a jug in incised ware, usually identified as Cycladic but possibly Anatolian.

Gamma 51 was a much younger man (**6**), only 28 when he died. He was one of the two final interments in Grave Gamma, the latest in the circle, which also contained remains of three earlier burials. He was once more a fine specimen: 'a tall particularly strong-boned, long bodied and large footed man with traces of injury, possibly a healed battle scar, by his left eye'. An oval hole in the top of his skull was the result of trepanation and two fractures lead away from the hole towards the front of the head, possibly the injuries that made the trepanation seem necessary. There no healing on the bone round the hole so the attempt would appear to have failed. Musgrave *et al.* see a family resemblance (though after several generations) between G 51 and Z 59. Though this man was only slightly younger than burial #1 (33 years old) he had far fewer grave goods, only two jugs, one large and one small, and three small drinking vessels, possibly because of his untoward death. The grave as a whole was very well equipped and exemplifies the multiple cultural strands at this period of transition from the Middle Bronze Age to the Late Bronze Age.

There was a clear differentiation in the grave goods apart from pottery between male and female burials. The men usually had a full set of weapons, both simple and elaborate, and some items of personal adornment. Women had pins, several of which were elaborate, and jewellery as well as some personal adornment. Grave Omicron which contained the rock crystal duck bowl, probably a Cretan imitation of an Egyptian original, was called the 'Princess' Grave' by the excavators. Much work has recently been done by Kilian-Dirlmeier and Dietz on the analysis of the contents of these graves and those of Grave Circle A.

The work of the Minoan-Mycenaean Food project has produced important information about the diet of those buried in the two grave circles. The skeletal remains of 22 of the 35 people from Grave Circle B were studied for evidence of their diet. As well as the general good health which had been previously noted, the striking result was that only the two eldest (thus including Pelops) had received as much as 10-20 per cent of their protein from the sea. In addition one of the four women tested had not enjoyed as much meat (and this includies animal derivatives like dairy products) as the rest of the sample.

It is particularly unfortunate that our knowledge of the Middle Bronze Age is so scrappy for this is the period when the fusion of the apparent newcomers with the existing population took place and laid the stalwart foundations of Mycenaean civilisation. It is in the later phases of the period that Mycenae itself takes over the leadership of the Argolid. The question 'Why Mycenae?' is much discussed.

5 The Early Palatial period

This period marks the beginning of the Mycenaean period proper but the evidence available for its interpretation is sadly skewed with the bulk coming from burials of three different kinds – a situation completely reversed in the next period. There is a vast increase in evident wealth and in ostentatious display in burials of all three kinds. The settlement on the other hand – both of the ordinary and the elite – lies on the whole deeply buried beneath the structures of the two phases of the subsequent period.

The Early Palatial period is generally marked by smaller 'early state modules' throughout central and southern Greece which later amalgamate (or are amalgamated forcibly) into the larger 'kingdoms' of the fourteenth and thirteenth centuries. It is hard to see exactly how Mycenae itself relates to this model of society. The site has become the leading one of the Argolid and possibly of the whole of southern Greece but its own internal structure is unclear, particularly the nature of the elite who are so obvious in the archaeological record.

Grave Circle A

Though in archaeological terms, both in date and style, Grave Circle A overlaps Grave Circle B, it can be taken to exemplify the cultural emergence that occurs at Mycenae in the seventeenth century BC. The graves appear to have held nine women, eight men and one child though there is some argument about one burial in shaft grave IV where the earliest burials occur. The latest tomb is shaft grave I which is only fractionally earlier than the first of the tholos tombs at Mycenae (and contemporary with the earliest chamber tombs). The bulk of the burials however are from LH IB, the first truly Mycenaean period in pottery terms (the same period as burial 4 of grave Gamma in Grave Circle B). As with the earlier circle, the goods accompanying the burials have differentiation between male and female, though jewellery and personal adornment are not confined to women. Weapon sets for men and pins for women are distinctive but many of the other grave goods occur with either. The overwhelming effect of Grave Circle A, however, is the vast quantity of wealth and the degree of craftsmanship which the grave goods exhibit (**colour plate 7**). The source of the wealth remains a matter of great discussion. There is not much pottery (as there are many metal vessels to take its place) but what there is shows the same range of origin as Grave Circle B with material from Crete and from the Cyclades as well as other areas of the

7 *Grave stelai from Grave A of Grave Circle B (recut as a base) and Grave V of Grave Circle A. Adapted by G.H. Norrie from Mylonas, GCB, and Karo, Schachtgräber*

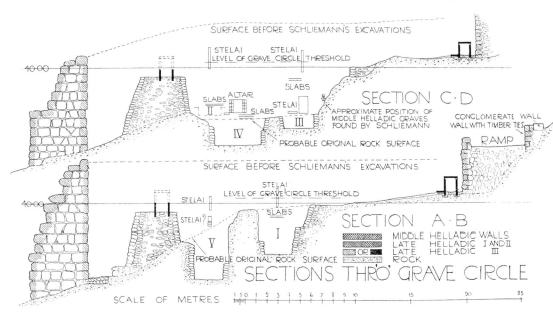

8 *Sections through Grave Circle A showing the pre-excavation surface and development in the Late Bronze Age.* © Mycenae Archive: Piet de Jong

9   *Patterning of ornaments from grave circle A and how they were designed.*
After Grundmann in Karo, Schachtgräber

mainland. The other grave goods are often of disputable origin: some are clearly Cretan and others Egyptian which almost certainly arrived via Crete. Many however seem to be by Cretan craftsmen working to the tastes and standards of the mainland chieftains. A distinctive feature of decoration in the shaft graves is the use of spiral patterns on ornaments (**9**) and on the grave stelai (**7**). This type of spiral is a legacy from the Early Bronze Age and does not occur on Crete. Of particular interest is a wooden bowl from shaft grave V which has been examined for dendrochronological dating. The result gives a *terminus post quem* of 1577 BC which suits conventional chronology.

Grave Circle A is also unique in other ways than wealth. Six shaft graves were constructed closely together on a rock slope adjacent to various areas which had been used for burials throughout the Middle Helladic period (**5**). A seventh lay nearby to the north but was not treated in later times with the respect accorded to the other six graves. A low wall which can be seen below the later enclosure wall on the west may be part of an original enclosure wall (**8**). Pieces of 13 decorated stelai (**7**) have been identified as well as several additional undecorated ones. Because in the later remodelling of the area the stelai seem to have faced west, i.e. away from the entrance to the grave circle, it is suggested that this may have been the original orientation which was preserved when they were raised to the new level. In this case the stelai would have faced out over the low wall toward the various approach routes to the citadel which ran along the lower west slope of the hill.

The respect with which these six graves were treated is striking. Though within the graves themselves the usual practices by which earlier burials were thrust to one side were used, the tombs as a whole were not disturbed and in the full Palatial period (in the first part of the thirteenth century) they were incorporated into a special monument that formed a focus of attention just within the new and imposing Lion Gate. Moreover a sherd of the early classical period found in the area of Grave Circle A bears the inscription 'To the hero' and there does not seem to have been any Hellenistic overbuilding of this area. This would suggest that the reverence in which it was held persisted and it is perhaps this same tradition that was told to Pausanias in the second century AD.

Who then are these 19 people? The number of burials and the fact that others are being buried at much the same time in similar but less rich tombs in Grave Circle B led to the suggestion that they were a group of warrior chieftains who display ostentatious wealth possibly to validate their claim to pre-eminence. Even though it would not take as long to construct as a tholos or chamber tomb, a large shaft grave would have had to be prepared during the lifetime of the first intended occupant and thus forms a definite form of image projection. It seems likely too that these families are also those who continued to display their position in the tholos tomb period which followed.

Tholos tombs

The Cyclopean Tomb, the earliest of the tholos tombs at Mycenae, can be dated, on the basis of the pottery found in it, to the LH IIA period (as indeed are six of the total nine). It thus is either contemporary with or follows very closely on the last of the shaft graves. Possibly Grave Circle A was still in use for one family group but others changed to the new type of tomb already in use in Messenia. The two tholoi near the acropolis, the Tomb of Aegisthus and the Lion Tomb, are the largest of their respective constructional groups and could have been built for members of the dominant faction. The reason for the change from shaft grave to tholos for high status burial may be purely one of convenience in reopening the tomb for subsequent burials or to give greater impact.

A tholos tomb has a circular stone-built chamber approached by a passage or dromos. One tholos, that at Kokla south of Argos, has the chamber built within a large rock cut vault like an enormous chamber tomb, but usually the chamber is built within a cylinder cut down into a hillside from above with the dromos cut in from the side. The masonry is corbelled and the whole was stabilised by a mound of earth heaped over the top. The recent restoration of the so-called Tomb of Aegisthus has given us much more information about the building of tholos tombs and their amazing engineering. It now seems likely that all tholoi had relieving triangles (**colour plate 22**) (despite the narrow overlap of the lintel blocks on the door jambs originally emphasised by Wace) though this cannot be proved for the Cyclopean Tomb and the Epano Phournos which are not preserved above the lintel. The stone for the dome was carefully cut and shaped on the spot (shown by layers of chips at different levels in the fill behind the dome) and the fill itself was amazingly clean and consistent in colour and texture. We have known for some time that the whole was carefully sealed by a cap of clay from the Plesia clay bed to the south. A simple manner of constructing such tombs has been suggested by Cavanagh and Laxton (**11**). The Tomb of Aegisthus combines features of both the first and second groups of tholoi, as a façade in poros stone was added sometime during the use of the tomb. This feature (which can be seen clearly in the Lion Tomb) would have added considerable visual impact to the monument.

Mycenae is unique for having nine tholos tombs, divided rather too neatly into three groups of three, each group consisting of one early, one middle and one late example (**12**). All of the first two groups as well as at least the first of the last group were constructed before the first stage of the fortification walls. Of the nine tombs at Mycenae five can be easily visited (marked by an ★ in the caption to **10**) but the others are often difficult to find on the confusing terraces of the west slopes of the Panagia ridge and beyond.

Unfortunately all the tholos tombs have been robbed and only small traces, largely pottery fragments, remained of the wealth they once contained. This phenomenon is not unique to Mycenae but is the case for almost all tholoi known. One grave in the tholos tomb at Vaphio in Laconia (where the famous gold cups were found) was not robbed and was fully published by Tsountas. It can be taken as an example of

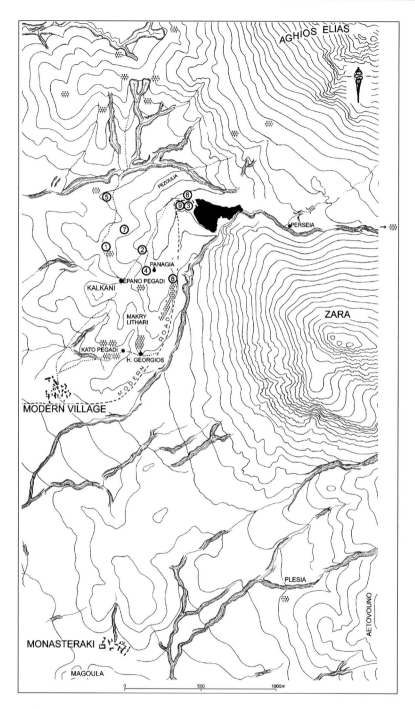

10 Area of Mycenae: the tholos tombs and the cemeteries of chamber tombs. © Mycenae
Archive. The tholos tombs in chronological order are: The Cyclopean Tomb (1), *The
Epano Phournos (2), *The Tomb of Aegisthus (3), The Panagia Tomb (4), The Kato
Phournos (5), *The Lion Tomb (6), The Tomb of the Genii (7), *The Treasury of
Atreus (8) and *The Tomb of Clytemnestra (9). Those marked * are easily visited

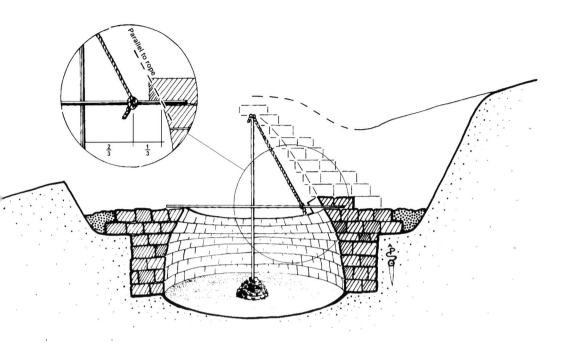

11   *Possible simple method of construction for a tholos tomb.*
     © Mycenae Archive: after Cavanagh and Laxton, BSA 76, 1981

EPANO PHOURNOS

KATO PHOURNOS

CLYTEMNESTRA

12   *Tholos tombs: an example of each chronological and constructional group.*
     © Mycenae Archive: Charles K. Williams II

what might have been. This was a single built cist in the northern part of the tholos. Near the western short side of the cist were: one sword, two spearheads, one inexplicable bronze object, six knives, one incense burner, one strainer, one silver bowl, one mirror, one razor, ten bronze discs, one tube of corrugated bronze sheet, five lead discs, two alabaster vases, a small silver spoon, two stone vases, two lamps, and four cups. Nearby were 80 amythest beads and two seals. Nearer to the northern long side were a dagger with gold ornaments on the handle and two silver cups. There were 24 seals symmetrically arranged towards the southern and northern walls. To the northern assemblage belong also a gold and a bronze ring, one shallow silver bowl [phiale] and two small silver objects. Two axes, a knife and four lead discs came from the eastern end of the cist.

Chamber tombs

The first usage of many of the 27 cemeteries of chamber tombs (**10**) can also be dated to this same period. A chamber tomb is rock cut and the positioning and size depend on the nature of the rock available. In plan they resemble tholos tombs with an entrance passage opening through a doorway into a chamber. There may be secondary chambers, niches, grave pits in the floor, and other elaborations. The Kalkani North group in particular, where 'horizontal stratigraphy' (lateral expansion of the cemetery through time) is obvious, but also the Souleimani group have tombs datable to LHIIA, and several groups have produced material as early as LH II in general terms. These tombs, though not as rich as the Vaphio grave, contain a wide range of handsome pottery (**13**) and valuable objects (**colour plates 8 & 9**). A chamber tomb was used for multiple burials presumably showing a kinship among the occupants. The cemeteries, like the groups of tholos tombs, may be taken to show the land holdings of wider clan groups among the population. It is, however, difficult to link the chamber tomb groups to the tholoi (**10**). One chamber tomb of the Alepotrypa group has the chamber itself cut to resemble a tholos even to the mark of a false cap stone – the next best thing? – and several have painted façades though none of these can be dated to the earliest phase.

The settlement and the acropolis

We know rather less about Early Palatial houses of this period but we do have evidence that there was settlement on the Panagia Ridge and in the Pezoulia area (**10**).

A central building, possibly the residence for a ruler (a 'maison de chef') like that suggested for Tiryns, existed on the summit of the acropolis, which stands high above the slopes on all sides except the west (**colour plate 1**). The evidence for this comes from the very high quality pottery found beneath later structures and from the fragments of fresco (with plant decoration) from the same source. There is little evidence on the mainland for structures of this date, but some idea of the general

13 *Decorated pottery of the Early Palatial period LH I – LH IIIA1.* © Mycenae Archive.
   a. Stage 1: LH I: settlement and tomb pottery accompanied by large pots and unpainted
      pots in styles derived from Middle Helladic. These small vessels are among the earliest
      examples of the Mycenaean dark-on-light style
   b. Stage 2 LH IIA: tomb pottery from the chamber tombs
   c. Stage 3 LH IIB – IIIA1: drinking vessels
   d. Stage 3 LH IIB – IIIA1: closed vessels of both settlement and tomb use
   All accompanied by large and unpainted vessels in all types of context
   e. Stage 3 LH II – IIIA1: drinking set with krater, jug and goblet

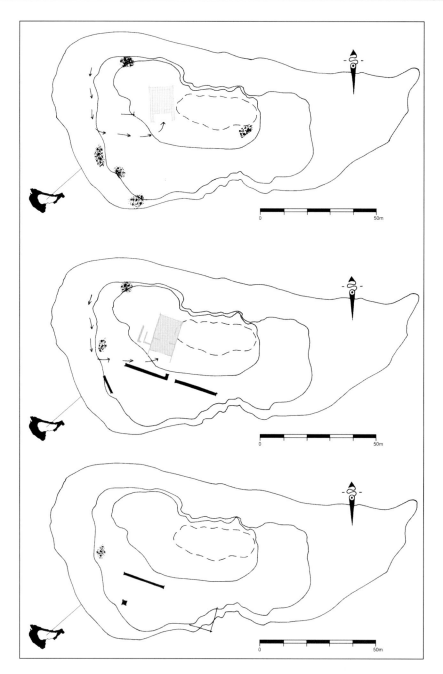

14 *The development of the palace during the Early Palatial and first part of the Palatial period.*
© Mycenae Archive.
Palace II (LH IIA) entry and megaron as suggested by Mylonas surrounded by dumps of high class pottery and food refuse
Palace III (LH IIB-IIIA1) suggested realignment of megaron with surviving walls of the complex and deposits of pottery
Palace IV (LH IIIA 2 late) traces of first stage of the Palatial complex discovered beneath the existing building: the first structure to use the extended terrace at the south-east

effect can be gained from the well-preserved and elaborately decorated houses at Akrotiri on Thera which are in general contemporary with Grave Circle A. There is no evidence for the plan of this early 'palace' but it is generally agreed that it must have followed the natural contours of the hill, unlike the following stages where the hill was adapted to suit an overall plan. Mylonas has suggested a possible layout (**14**). Five deposits of this high quality 'domestic' refuse have been found on the upper slopes of the acropolis hill and are thus likely to have originated from this building and not to have been brought uphill for disposal. The heavily burnt debris included as well as pottery and fresco fragments, much animal bone (sheep and pig) with copious amounts of oyster and mussel shells. We can perhaps picture our chieftains, richly adorned, feasting in a frescoed hall on the summit of the acropolis. Certainly the evidence for diet from the Minoan-Mycenaean Food project suggests that the men of Grave Circle A ate marine products while the one woman tested did not.

A stout wall just below the north-west corner of the later palace was thought to be a Middle Helladic fortification wall but from the sherds found in it, it must date from Early Palatial times. It is not necessarily a fortification wall but could well be an outer demarcation for the structures on the summit.

Religion

Evidence for religious practice does not come from Mycenae itself but from a site just east of Epidaurus where there is a later sanctuary to Apollo Malleatis. Here on a built terrace there is an outdoor altar. Nearby were dedications, in a large pit (below the later altar) among layers of ash: small cups of the so-called Vaphio type, the ubiquitous plain handleless bowls and double axes cut from thin sheet gold. This sanctuary does not share the full range of features of a Minoan peak sanctuary and at present remains something of a tantalising enigma. Mycenaean religion, it would seem, from this very beginning of the real Mycenaean period, borrowed the trappings of Minoan cult but not necessarily the full range of practice or probably belief.

Overseas contacts

The spread of trade or contact is extremely wide (**15**) though the exact nature of the relationship between the mainland and Crete is obscure. The idea of Cretan domination of the mainland has long been abandoned but there is clear and extensive cultural influence. This may be the result of imitation of actual imported elite goods or reflect the movement of craftsmen.

There is also the enigma of Tomb Rho. This is a built tomb from within the confines of Grave Circle B but we have no idea whether or not the builder knew of the existence of the grave circle when the tomb was planned. Architecturally the most obvious parallels for this tomb are from sites like Ugarit and its port Minet el Beida but these are all of later date – though archaeologists working in the area are

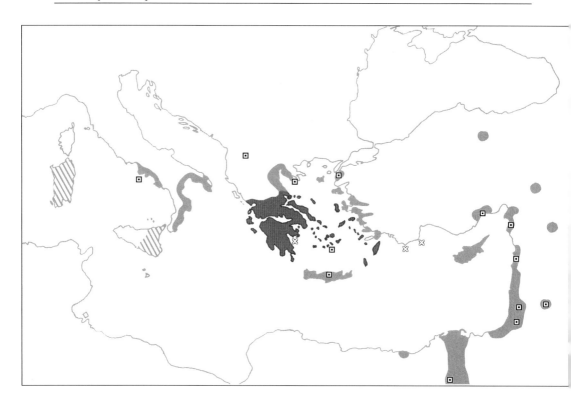

15   *Mycenaean contacts and influence in the Mediterranean: Early Palatial marked by
     symbols and Palatial with light shading; the core area of Mycenaean culture shaded
     dark. X marks the three Bronze Age wrecks*

confident that the type is of long standing in the Levant. There is, however, another
parallel: the Temple Tomb at Knossos which is unfortunately now destroyed. It was
more elaborate but of almost exactly the same date. For whomsoever it was built,
Tomb Rho remains a very tangible proof of some kind of foreign influence at the
heart of Mycenae.

As usual the most easily traced export product is pottery. In the west, there are
high quality cups of the 'Vaphio' shape (**13** top left) on the island of Vivara off the
coast by Naples. Similar pots have been found in Albania and at Torone on the west
side of the central peninsula of Chalcidice in Macedonia as well as at Akrotiri on
Thera. To the east, a handsome goblet slightly later in date was dedicated in the Fosse
Temple at Lachish (and a sherd of another similar vessel has just (12/00) been identified from the same context), a 'palace style' vase was found in the temple under
Amman airport and other high quality pieces have been found in Egypt, notably near
the Teti pyramid at Sakhara. (These last are of particular chronological importance.)
Exotic raw materials were imported though we cannot say whether they arrived
regularly and directly from the source area, whether we have the remains of unique
shipments that were carefully hoarded, distributed and recycled or a steady trickle of

down-the-line trade. Ostrich eggs, ivory and gold originated in Nubia, amber in the Baltic, lapis lazuli in Afganistan. The relation between the amber spacer beads of the Wessex culture and the ones from grave O of Grave Circle B is unclear but a fact. Tin was more essential but its source is still a matter for debate with Cornwall, the Taurus mountains in Turkey, Afganistan and the Carpathian mountains all suggested.

The pottery cannot have been the only export, though it is noticeable that at this period the exports of it are of handsome well-decorated pieces probably of value in themselves, many of them open vessels without contents. This contrasts with the bulk of exports in the full Palatial period (**28c**). It is generally supposed that there were also exports invisible in the archaeological record for which some documentary evidence can be adduced. Weapons, textiles and even sandals as well as pottery are mentioned as coming from 'Crete' (Kaptara/Caphtor which may of course imply only the intermediary) in a text from Mari (of the eighteenth century BC) in exchange for tin.

The last phases of the Early Palatial period (LH IIIA1 in pottery terms – the early fourteenth century) saw an even greater expansion of overseas contacts and it seems likely that many of the markets exploited in the Palatial period were explored and established at this time.

6 The Palatial period

This is the Mycenaean period proper, the acme of Mycenaean civilisation, covering the archaeological phases LH IIIA and LH IIIB, in hard dates the fourteenth and thirteenth centuries BC (**1**). This period sees the climax of the influence of Mycenae itself and is often called the Palatial period, echoing the terminology initiated by Greek scholars for Crete and the reality of the palatial bureaucracy under which the mainland was governed – a situation which we have come to appreciate in the last 50 years since the decipherment of the Linear B script by Michael Ventris.

The period develops directly without any cultural break from the preceding one and in the pottery terms, by which we so often have to define the distinctions between chronological phases, it is hard to determine exactly where, for instance, LH IIB ends and LH IIIA1 starts. Two particular features are clear: first the characteristics which separate mainland Greek from Cretan culture become ever more apparent and secondly mainland Greek influence begins to spread even more widely, particularly in the eastern Mediterranean.

At Mycenae itself the period includes the structures at which the visitor has marvelled throughout the millennia – the fortifications and the Treasury of Atreus – but also the Palace itself as we know it, the other two tholos tombs of the last group and most of the 'houses' that are visible to today's tourist. It seems likely that the rulers of Mycenae used a corvée system of labour and we can even suggest in some detail how the work force was deployed over time. From the table (**1**) we see that the Treasury of Atreus was the first of the major monuments of this period to be built. It may be easier however for the reader if the discussion is by the type of monument and their whereabouts rather than strictly chronological and I shall therefore deal with the citadel and the town before the tombs. More detailed description of the individual monuments inside the walls is given separately in chapter 7.

Building technique developed significantly during these two centuries, notably in about 1325 BC. In particular there started a system of constructing artificial terraces both to extend the area available for building and to strengthen the foundations of major structures. Such terraces required advances in drainage; water was allowed to seep through to be channelled out by built drains through the outer terrace walling. In the case of the citadel wall the drains were carefully built narrowing at the outlet so that the press of water would keep the exit clear. We cannot tell whether these techniques developed because of a shortage of space or because of damage to existing structures, perhaps from earthquake. Much of what we still see, however, is the result. These terraces were usually built in compartments for strength and filled with relatively small stones (known to the excavators as potatoes) mixed with soil and

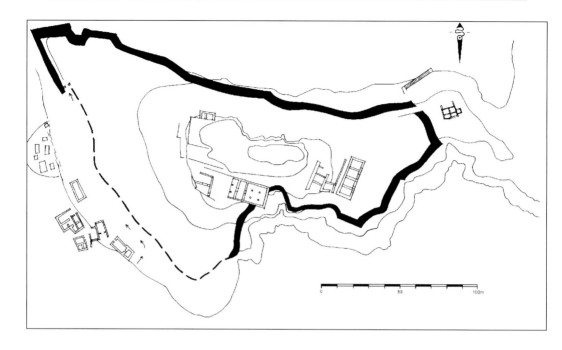

16 *The first stage of the fortifications (LH IIIA2-B1) with the structures known or suggested to exist in that period. The line suggested for the west wall lies on the 250m contour.* © Mycenae Archive

domestic rubbish, largely pottery. This pottery was probably brought from rubbish dumps elsewhere but with the stones forms a very useful component in the fill, particularly from the point of view of bulk and of drainage. Obviously these collections of pottery will have built up as dumps over a number of years but the build up will cease abruptly when they are sealed in the terrace fill. The copious pottery evidence from these terraces has enabled a detailed sequence to be established for the fourteenth and early thirteenth centuries BC.

The citadel

Fortifications

Fortification of the citadel is usually thought to have taken place in three stages. Of the first stage (**16**) only the north wall and part of the south wall remain; that on the west (suggested along the 250m contour) was demolished when the present west wall was built. Similarly the east wall was partially demolished when the North–east Extension was constructed.

This first fortification can be dated, by sherds found low in the fill of the north wall, to the second half of the fourteenth century. The main gate was probably, as later, at the north–west corner but is thought to have faced in the opposite direction.

17 *Tools available to*
    Mycenaean builders and
    craftsmen: the pendulum
    saw and the bow drill as
    well as axe and adze blades.
    © Mycenae Archive

18 *The Anastylosis*
    Service reconstructing
    the Citadel Wall.
    Lucas Benachi 1950s

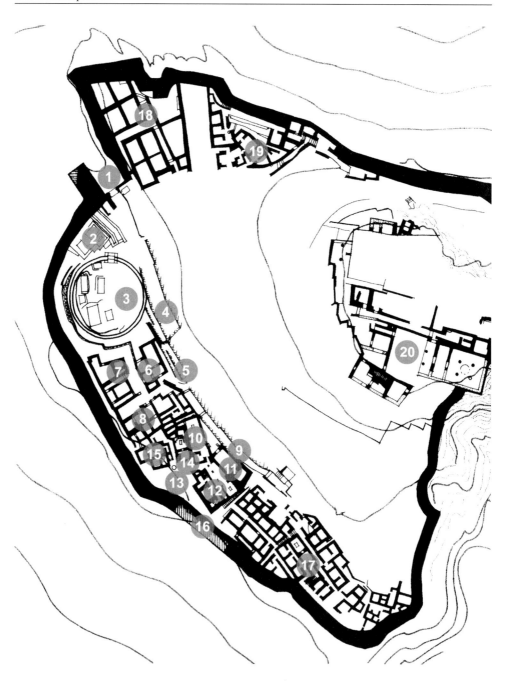

19 Excavated structures inside the Citadel. © Mycenae Archive
   1. Lion Gate; 2. Granary; 3. Grave Circle A; 4. Great Ramp; 5. Little Ramp;
   6. Ramp House; 7. House of the Warrior Vase; 8. South House (with its annex to the
   east); 9. Processional Way; 10. Megaron; 11. Shrine Gamma; 12. Tsountas' House;
   13. Central Court; 14. Temple; 15. Room with the Fresco; 16. Hellenistic Tower,
   possibly overlying the West Gate; 17. South-west Quarter; 18. North Quarter;
   19. House M; 20. Palace; 21. Artisans' Quarter; 22. House of Columns;
   23. House Delta; 24. House Gamma; 25. North Storerooms;
   26. North or Postern Gate; 27. Underground Cistern; 28. North sally port;
   29. South sally port; 30. House Alpha; 31. House Beta

It would have been approached by a road from the south-west from a crossing of the stream bed identified by Mylonas and reached by the ramps rising from south to north which were discovered beneath the later Great Ramp. The North or Postern Gate in its present form is later but a narrow entrance at the north-east corner, through which the populace could have reached the water sources to the east, is suggested by Mylonas. The line of this first fortification follows the contour of the rock exactly; this is particularly noticeable just east of the north-west corner where there is a sharp indentation. In the second stage of building such indentations were bridged. The blocks are large roughly shaped chunks of limestone without mortar but with small stones in the interstices. They are so large that the construction of the wall was assigned to the mythical giants, the Cyclopes. We do not know for certain how the walls were built but recent studies (see bibliography) have suggested methods by which the construction could have been accomplished and emphasise the importance of the invention of the pendulum saw (**17**). The large limestone blocks of the walls average two tons and would apparently have needed at least four men to manoeuvre them. As the citadel of Mycenae (as well as the hills on either side of it) is largely composed of limestone the blocks could have been cut near where they were to be used but there is no positive evidence of this. Earth ramps would have allowed the blocks to be manoeuvred into place from below. When we watched the work of the Anastylosis repairing the walls in the 1950s (**18**) we came to realise that hard labour was more important than elaborate equipment. In both phases the Cyclopean masonry is only a façade on either side and the core of the wall is a rubble fill. We do not know how the wall was finished on top. It would have been quite wide enough for a walkway with a narrow protective parapet on the outer edge possibly of mudbrick. The finished wall had a thickness of 7-7.5m and the stone section was probably some 12.5m high (to judge from the Hellenistic Tower, built later into the west section, where we know the exact height).

The second stage (**19**), usually dated to the mid-thirteenth century, added some of the most important features of the site: the Lion Gate with its conglomerate surround, a newly aligned ramp leading to the summit and a new west wall encircling a refurbished grave circle. This stage of the walls is differentiated from the first by the method of building. Not only is conglomerate widely used at key points to give a contrasting effect to the basic limestone, but the foundations now have a bedding of Plesia clay and often of small stones which enabled the large blocks to be settled into place more easily. This change is probably due to the different nature of the rock on which the west wall is built. Quarries for conglomerate exist at the edge of the modern village and on the lower slopes of Agios Elias. Thus though it had to be brought from slightly further away it was differently worked, by hammering or, for a fine surface, by sawing. Both the limestone and conglomerate would have been pale buff when newly cut and the fine glistening surface of fresh cut conglomerate may have contributed to the epithet of Golden Mycenae.

It is almost impossible to work out exactly the sequence in which and date at which these major features were constructed. The dating is based first on the obvious architectural history (which walls abut against pre-existing ones etc.) or, when this is not apparent, on the very small quantities of pottery which can be retrieved from underneath the walls or from their core fill. As this pottery in any case gives only a *terminus post quem* − a date *after* which the sherds found their way into such a secondary context − accuracy is difficult. We can only suggest what seems to make sense but the building sequences suggested here are not universally accepted and may well be overturned by new evidence. Following probably almost immediately on the work at the west, a third and last phase of the fortifications comprised the alterations at the north-east of the citadel: the North Gate and the North-east Extension. The latter is thought to have been built solely in order to bring the entrance to the underground cistern within the walls. Two passages through the walls, a narrow one to the north and a wider one to the south were included in this extension. All the features here are usually dated to the end of the thirteenth century.

There is an alternative possibility. The pottery from the destruction level of House Beta within the North-east Extension appears to belong to the earthquake horizon of the third quarter of the thirteenth century and can certainly not belong to a period *after* the end of the thirteenth century. Moreover the relation between the west corridor of this house and its entrance and the retaining wall of the cistern is problematic. It might be suggested that this house was originally built before the North-east Extension. This leads to the idea that the cistern itself might also antedate the extension. In that case the descent would have begun further to the north (**16**) and been approached from the exit at the north of the citadel. House Beta could still have been concerned with administration of the water source but become damaged in the earthquake, necessitating the repairs and changes, including the building of the North-east Extension, which did take place towards the end of the century.

The palace

It is clear that there were at least two building phases in the structure we see today but as this structure cannot have been built until after the citadel wall formed the terrace which supports it at the south-east corner, there must have been an earlier 'palace' following the destruction of the building of the Early Palatial period from which we have the widespread burnt deposits. We assume that the supporting wall at the south-east corner belongs to the first stage of the fortifications because of the heavy indentation at this point and because the date of this first stage of the palace cannot be as late as the second phase of the walls. There is no pottery evidence to date the construction of an early fourteenth-century palace but at least two walls may be assigned to it: a wall lying behind the later north wall of the Great Court along the south side of the south corridor together with the original layout at the east end of this corridor and the so-called 'old wall' − an irregularly built section of the west terrace wall (**14 & 21**). As these two are not in alignment no overall plan can be put forward but Mylonas suggests a megaron on the top of the hill aligned with the south corridor. Two pottery deposits are also associated with this phase.

As can be seen from the air view (**20**) the area of the Palace is now very heavily denuded but a plan can be suggested for the various phases. The distinctive evidence for an earlier phase of the Palace standing today, which must have almost

20 *Palace V of the late thirteenth century superimposed on a balloon photograph of the existing remains.* Photograph © 1994 J. Wilson Myers and Eleanor E. Myers; overlay © Mycenae Archive

totally destroyed what had existed here in the early part of the Palatial period, is scanty but clear: the Pillar Basement which was later filled in (**14 & 22**). The construction date in the last quarter of the fourteenth century is based upon the sherds found beneath the floor of the Pillar Basement and must have followed closely on the building of the citadel wall which supported the new south terrace. This building made use of the south corridor but adapted the south end and reused a set of handsome blocks in poros stone in the construction of a main drain below the Great Court.

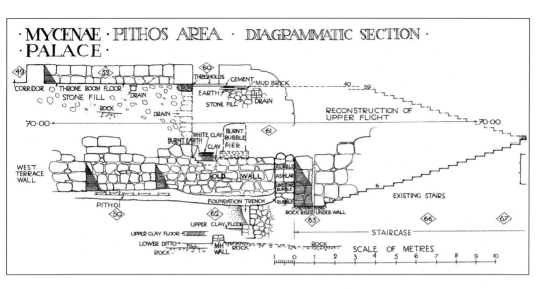

21 Palace: diagrammatic section of the Pithos area and the Grand Staircase. The numbers in diamonds refer to the room/area numbering on the detailed plan published in BSA XXV and Wace 1949. © Mycenae Archive: Piet de Jong 1920s

The basic plan of this Palace seems to have consisted of three blocks divided by long corridors (**20**). One approach was from the north-west corner through a Propylon and a passageway from which the access corridors could be reached. The northern, and thus the cooler, terrace would have had basements for storage with an upper terrace of rooms which would catch the breeze (compare the plan of the site museum). The central part of the middle terrace seems to have been open as a sort of central court overlooked by the rooms to the north. The east end of this portion was approached not from the south corridor but apparently only from the porch to the Megaron. It is therefore suggested that the private quarters of the ruler lay here but all details of the plan are now gone. The southern block contained the large reception rooms: a courtyard with a porch on the eastern side backed by a shallow lobby and the Megaron with central hearth surrounded by four columns. On analogy with Pylos and Tiryns a throne would have stood in the middle of the south wall. The east end of this part of the complex was built on an artificial terrace supported by the citadel wall which extended the space available at the south-east corner. But it was this section that later fell and was only restored in the middle of the last century. To the west of the court lay a suite of rooms once interpreted as another throne room but now thought to be a guest suite (on analogy with the layout of the palace of Nestor at Pylos).

This suite lies over the Pillar Basement (**21**) and must date from the last building phase but other rooms of probably comparable plan would have stood over the basement before it was filled in. The in-fill seems to have followed a calamity in which these main rooms were gutted by fire, as the nature of the debris and marks

59

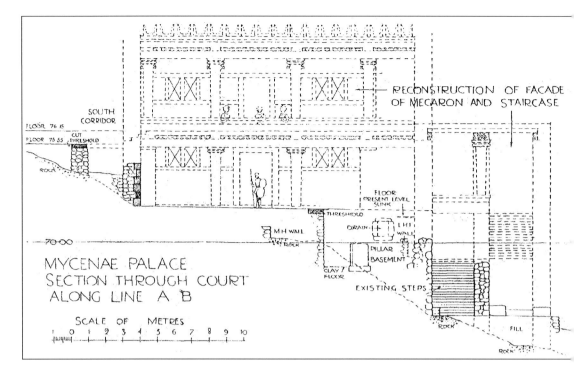

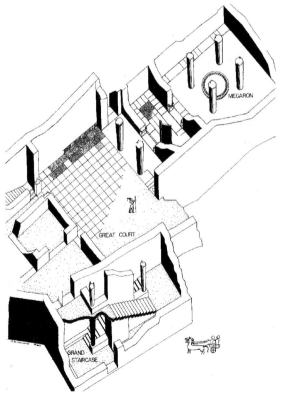

22 Palace: section through the Great Court and Grand Staircase. © Mycenae Archive: Piet de Jong 1920s

23 Palace: the approach to the State Rooms. © Mycenae Archive: Charles K. Williams II

on the ashlar blocks of the north wall of the court shows. The reconstruction included the in-fill of the Pillar Basement and a new floor for the courtyard. The wall paintings, burnt and otherwise, were removed from the walls (as at Tiryns) and new ones installed. It is probable that this calamity was caused by earthquake – which often leads to fire damage where there are open hearths and wood in the construction. It is somewhat surprising that the roofless courtyard was now floored in painted stucco which would not have lasted long. Indeed it did not have the chance to last, as the building was soon to be gutted again by fire.

The last feature of the palace complex to be built was the Grand Staircase. It is not on the same alignment as the blocks of the Palace but lies at an angle against the south-west corner of the complex (**20-23**). It is uncertain whether or not there was an earlier approach here which this replaced but the alignment is surely related to the underlying contour of the rock. The ordinary entrance to the palace area would have been from the north-west at all periods. Consideration of the overall plan of the citadel (**19**) shows how close this approach to the palace is to the Cult Centre by the west wall. It may be suggested that the elaborate Processional Way leading east from the Cult Centre formed part of the alterations that followed the building of the west extension of the citadel wall and linked the area to the Grand Staircase of the Palace.

East wing (*19*)

Three further terraces lay to the east of the main palace structure. On these lay other buildings of the overall palace complex. The upper two terraces which are now almost completely denuded were divided from the third by a corridor (the east corridor) running from south to north. On this third terrace lay the Artisans' Quarter, a structure of an unusual large rectangular plan in which a very considerable amount of raw materials and workshop debitage was found. The central feature of this building was a long narrow open court flanked on either side by corridors or porticoes off which opened a series of small rectangular rooms. On the west where the rock was higher these were built on an in-filled terrace while at the east the additional depth allowed by the lower rock level gave space for basement storerooms (**24**). The resemblance of the plan to that of souks of medieval times is probably not fortuitous.

Also considered part of the east wing is the House of Columns, another building of unusual plan but in this case apparently a residence of high status and quality. The house was entered from the north through an imposing doorway into a long corridor leading to an open court with the columns from which the house is named. A small door to one side off the entrance passage connected directly with the Artisans' Quarter. Opening onto the court were a pair of large rooms from one of which there was access to a stair and at least one small room. The plan resembles that of the small megaron complex at Tiryns but intriguingly it can also be used to illustrate the setting for the events at Odysseus' palace as described in the Odyssey, particularly the passage beside the megaron. The south part of the house was on three levels of which the basements at least were devoted to storage and bureau-

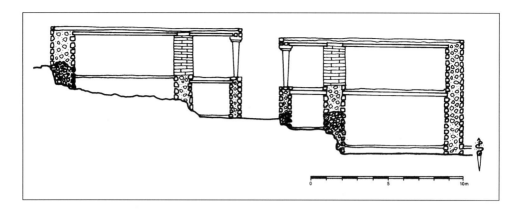

24 *Section west to east through the Artisans' Quarter.* After Mylonas 1966

cratic storage at that, for from them come some of the few examples of the Linear B script from within the citadel at Mycenae: two inscribed Stirrup Jars, and a clay tablet listing 'cloths of ko-u-ra type' (the exact meaning is still opaque). The inner parts of the house are constructed on a vast terrace, free standing within the citadel wall. This is dated by sherds in it and seems to date from after the citadel wall, despite the obvious difficulty of construction.

When the east wing is included, the palace complex as a whole measures just under 110,000ft^2 (1ha) and can be seen to surpass in overall extent the other two mainland palace complexes with restorable plans (Tiryns and Pylos are both about 55,000ft^2, 6,000m^2). None of the mainland palaces compares with that at Knossos (120,000ft^2 or 13,000m^2) though this would still have been functioning in the first phase of the Palatial period on the mainland, and in fact may have been under very strong mainland influence if not hegemony.

The palace at Tiryns like that at Mycenae has been heavily denuded and we can tell little about the specific function of any of its rooms. The situation at Pylos is completely different. Here we have destruction deposits of pottery in many rooms, including vast quantities of stored unpainted pottery and we have an archive room and an archive large enough to give us some idea of how the palace functioned as an administrative centre. This aspect of Mycenae will be discussed below (p.123) but here we may speculate where in the palace complex at Mycenae an archive room might have been situated. On the analogy with Pylos the obvious candidate is the so-called 'guardroom' just by the north-west entrance. Several deposits of unpainted pottery were found at various places within the Palace in spite of the nature of the remains and a row of specialist storerooms with large pithoi and much other pottery came to light on the north side of the citadel approached from the North Gate – the pithoi, because they had been mended with lead clamps, are thought to have contained cereals or dried fruit rather than liquids. A single but large Linear B tablet (recording barley, flour and cyperus) accompanied these finds (**61**). This position, both facing north and approached from this gate, would have suited the storage of produce brought in from the cereal growing areas to the north-east of the site.

Other structures

Most of the other structures within the citadel walls can be assigned to this period. The difficulties are to identify buildings from the earliest phases of the period and to put them all into any kind of order of construction. There is surprisingly little evidence for anything built within the walls between 1450 and 1300 BC. Almost the only good evidence that we have is the fresco sequence from below the Ramp House on the west slope which comes presumably from the building of which a few walls were found within the terrace of the later house. All other material found in the terraces and beneath buildings of the later phase is extremely scanty consisting of fragments of walls and a very few pots at best. A handsome cup from the Artisans' Quarter is a rare example of a complete late fourteenth-century pot from the citadel.

Of the main period, i.e. the thirteenth century, structures are preserved on all the slopes of the citadel hill. Many were almost completely excavated by Tsountas at the end of the nineteenth century and even then had been heavily damaged by over-building of the Hellenistic period. Recent painstaking work by Mylonas and by Iakovides has been able to clarify the plans and find some traces of chronological evidence. This evidence has not yet been published in detail though a programme of study has started. The overall picture (which study may well adjust) is that many were built in the years following the completion of the first citadel wall. Like the Palace they suffered damage in the second half of the thirteenth century, possibly from earthquake, and were repaired. Many seem to have suffered a burnt destruction around the end of the century and all seem to go out of use at this point. Reoccupation, if any, is distinct and at a higher level.

The west slope is different as it was not enclosed by the first stage of the fortifications. Here the building under the Ramp House and probably the Ramp House itself were built before the west wall was completed. The South House rests on a very heavy terrace. It is as monumental as that beneath the House of Columns and is probably only slightly earlier in date – about 1260 BC in round figures – but in this case its formidable construction may indicate that the house was built outside the citadel wall. The House of the Warrior Vase was built later than the South House and Grave Circle A but probably only shortly after the latter. Also on the west slope was the Cult Centre (**33**) which is the one area within the citadel not to have been excavated at all before 1953. The cult usage seems to have started before the citadel wall was built and to have been linked to the roadways approaching the citadel from the south-west. The earliest of the structures was Shrine Gamma (11) on the upper terrace. By the time the full group of shrines had been built in the middle of the thirteenth century, the complex comprised as well as Shrine Gamma, another large room on the higher level (the Megaron 10) with extensive storage basements, and, at a lower level around a central open space, two more shrines (the Temple complex 14 and the Room with the Fresco complex 15) and opposite them a large well-built house (Tsountas' House 12). The complex could also be approached from the Ramp House at the north along a poros stone causeway and a covered corridor (**31**).

Later the orientation of one of the lower buildings, the Room with the Fresco, was completely altered so that it was entered not from the open court but from the west. Not long after this (in archaeological terms) the citadel wall was built and this west entrance would have become very difficult of access – but this does not seem to have been something that mattered to the Mycenaeans as the plan of the lower town at Tiryns testifies. However a handsome approach (the Processional Way) to the whole area from the Palace directly down the west slope from the new Grand Staircase was built either now or in the reconstruction period after the earthquake.

The excavation evidence shows that about 1230 BC the whole area suffered a vast destruction, from the debris of which pottery and other cult items were not removed. From various signs such as the awe with which these cult items were treated, the patching in convenient pisé and the general nature of the damage, this destruction is thought to be the result of earthquake. Afterwards the whole area was tidied and patched up and most of the shrines were put back into use. But the Room with the Fresco complex was sealed off and not reused, possibly because access to it had become difficult if not impossible. Finally the whole area was destroyed by a devastating fire which turned the mudbrick walls solid and the stone foundations almost into rock.

The town

The survey carried out by the British School at Athens with the Archaeological Society in the early 1990s consolidated and expanded our knowledge of the settlement outside the citadel walls. Unfortunately only a few of the residential and commercial complexes of the whole area have been excavated but surface indications show us the area and to some extent the density of settlement. The area was some 80 acres (32 ha) but the density is debatable. A figure of up to 200 people per hectare is often suggested but this implies a closer density than the evidence seems to allow. At present we have little idea of an accurate extent for the town at either Tiryns or Pylos. What is clear from the results of the survey is that the suggestion that the settlement as a whole was composed of a series of sub-settlements or villages (each with its own cemetery) must be abandoned. The settlement area and the cemeteries are distinct.

The plan (**25**) shows the area of the town and the structures in it which have been excavated. The Panagia Ridge and the slope below it to the east carry the most imposing of the residences; commercial establishments have been found on the north-west on the Pezoulia slope while there are many smaller establishments throughout the area. The boundaries of the town seem to have been definitively marked and apparently officially established by the late fourteenth century – about the time the citadel itself is first walled. Apart from the tholos tombs, only one tomb lies within the area of the town. This is a chamber tomb immediately south of Grave Circle B, the use of which is assigned by the excavator to LH III A and B. What seems to be the cutting for the dromos of another chamber tomb lay under the

1 *Air view of Mycenae from the west.* Mycenae Archive: R.V. Schoder S.J.

2 *Mycenae (from the south-west) 7am 31 March 1849, watercolour by Edward Lear.* Gennadaius Library, Athens

3 Tiryns and Argos from the south-east. D.H. French 1957

4 Berbati valley from the south. D.H. French 1957

5 *Mycenae from the south-west.* Mycenae Archive: E.B. French 1954

6 *View across the Argive Plain from the Palace.* Mycenae Archive: E.B. French 1955

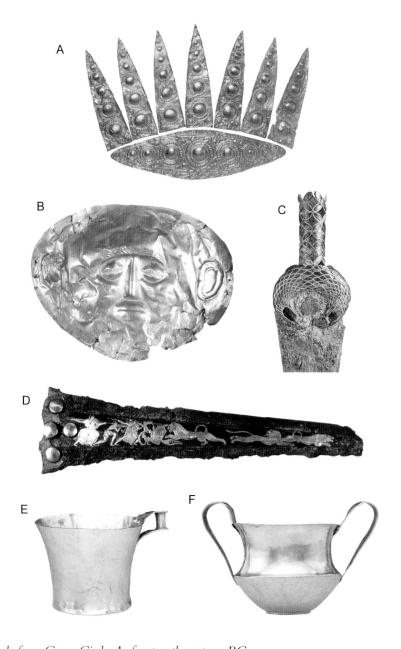

7 *Finds from Grave Circle A, fourteenth century BC.*
National Museum, Athens, arranged G.H. Norrie.
A: Crown from shaft grave III (NM 3+5); width 25.6in (65cm). The other way up this has been interpreted as decoration for a belt with pendants; B: Gold mask from shaft grave IV (NM 253); width 10.8in (27.5cm); C: Bronze sword with enamelled hilt from shaft grave IV (NM 294); length of hilt 2.5in (6.3cm); D: Bronze Dagger with scene of Lion Hunt in gold, electrum, silver and a black bronze alloy (NM 394) from shaft grave IV; length 9.33in (23.7cm); E: Gold cup (NM 630) from shaft grave V; height 3.75in (9.5cm); F: Gold cup (NM 440) from shaft grave IV; height with handles 4.5in (11.5cm)

8 *Jewellery from the chamber tombs now in the National Museum, Athens.*
Mycenae Archive: Piet de Jong.
Early Palatial: *Top: T518: 67,68,71 Beads of stone, glass and faience; Centre:*
T529:36 Stone pendant beads
Palatial: *Bottom: T526: 1,2 Egyptian scarabs of the 19th Dynasty, 5 amber beads,*
7 beads of elaborate glass mounted with lantern and disk bead of faience.
[This tomb contained only one skeleton and no grave goods except the jewellery and the
date of the jewellery is therefore difficult to establish except in relation to the scarabs which
are probably the latest items]

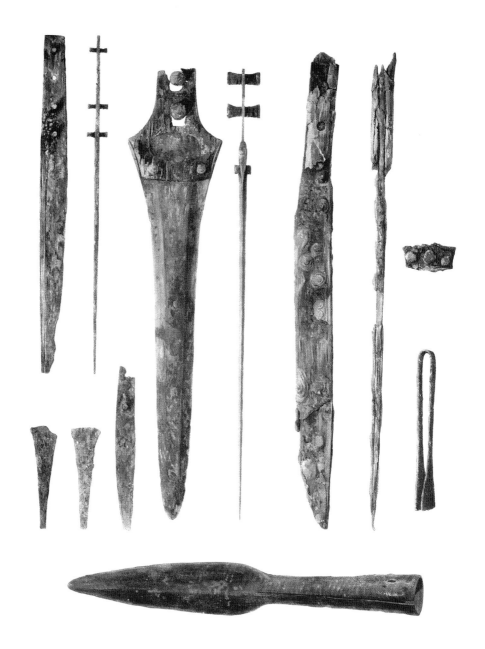

9 *Bronzes mainly from the chamber tombs now in the National Museum, Athens, early*
Palatial Period. Mycenae Archive: Piet de Jong
A: Knife, Tomb 518:50; length existing 7.4in (18.75cm); B: Dagger, Tomb 518:49;
length 10in (25cm); C: Knife, Tomb 529:25; length 10.6in (27cm); D: Dagger
fragment, Tomb 529:27; width 1.2in (3cm); E: Tweezers (once with wooden handle),
Tomb 529:26; length 2.2in (5.6cm); F: Knife, Tomb 518:51; length 3.66in (9.3cm);
G: Tweezers, Tomb 529:28; length 3.5in (8.8cm); H: Trial pit to south-west of
Acropolis (1920s excavations); length 8.27in (21cm)

10 *Wall-painting from beneath the House of the Oil Merchant, late fourteenth century BC showing a sedan chair with porter.* Mycenae Archive: Piet de Jong

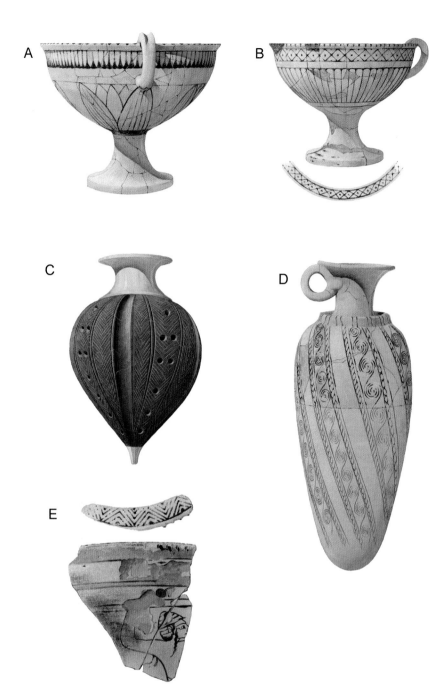

11 *Exotica from the House of Shields, early thirteenth century BC.*
Mycenae Archive: Piet de Jong
A: Faience goblet 55-216, NM 7515; height 5.2in (13cm); B: Faience goblet 53-311, NM 7505; height 5.2in (13cm); C: Ostrich egg rhyton of steatite (suggested faience at rim and base) 54-405 NM 7390; height 6.7in (17cm); D: Faience rhyton 54-416 NM 7510; height 7.85in (20cm); E: Faience rhyton with warrior 54-417 NM 7511; height 3.15in (8cm)

12 *Wall-painting from the Cult Centre, Room with the Fresco, thirteenth century BC.*
Mycenae Archive: Anneke Poelstra–Traga

13 *(and 14) Ivory from the Cult Centre,*
Room with the Fresco, thirteenth century
BC. Mycenae Archive: W.D.
Taylour. *Head of ?Deity 69-42 MM*
2001/62; height 2.66in (6.8cm)

14 *Lion with socket underneath for*
mounting on ?furniture 68-1191 MM
2001/63; length 7in (17.7cm)

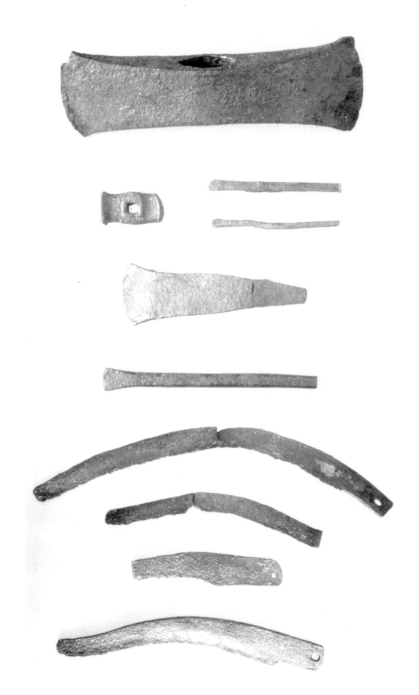

15   *Hoard of bronze implements from near the Poros Wall to east of the Tomb of Clytemnestra,*
thirteenth century BC. Mycenae Archive: Alison Franz
A: Double axe 52-423 NM 7660; length 8.66in (22cm); B: Small hammer 52-413
NM 7653; length 1.8in (4.6cm); C: Drill? 52-418 NM 7655; length 3.66in (9.3cm);
D: Fine chisel 52-416 NM 7655; length 3.8in (9.6cm); E: Large chisel 52-415 NM
7655; length 6.1in (15.5cm); F: Adze 52-410 NM 7650; length 5.7in (14.5cm);
G: Sickles 52-401,402,404,405 NM 7646; length 11.4in > 4.5in (29 > 11.5cm)

16   The South House Annex from the north. Diana Wardle

17   Egyptian faience plaque with the cartouche of Amenhotep III from the Room with the Fresco in the Cult Centre (68-1000 MM 18340; scale = 1.2in, 5cm).
Mycenae Archive: Jane Cocking

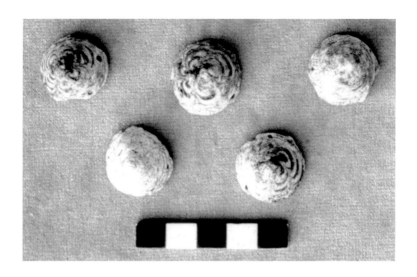

18   *Glass beehive beads from the Shrine in the Cult Centre (Selection of 69-1226, MM 18345>52, Scale = 1.2in, 5cm).* Mycenae Archive: W.D. Taylour

19   *Steatite mould for glass and gold jewellery from a storage area adjacent to the Cult Centre (66-1708 MM 17742; length 4in, 10.2cm).* E.B. French

20   The Warrior Vase
     (NM 1426)

21   View from burial platform
     at Khania to Mycenae.
     E.B. French 1987

22   Tomb of Aegisthus under restoration, to show newly revealed relieving triangle.
E.B. French 1998

*23 (and 24) Hoard of Hellenistic silver coins from a house to the east of the Perseia
Fountain House (see Dengate BSA 69) (39-117>125 MM 55886>94).*
Mycenae Archive: T. Leslie Shear Jnr. *Above, obverse; below, reverse*

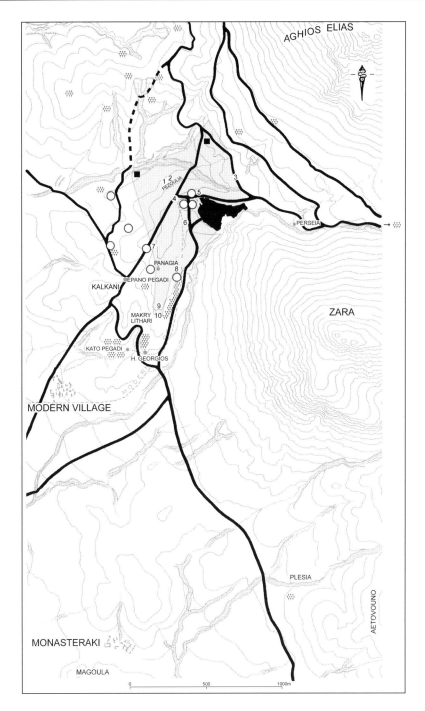

25 Area of Mycenae: excavated structures of the town and the road system in the
immediate vicinity of the site. © Mycenae Archive.
1 Cyclopean Terrace Building & House of the Wine Merchant; 2 Petsas' House;
3 Plakes House; 4 Houses by the modern car park; 5 Museum site; 6 Ivory Houses;
7 Lisa's House; 8 Panagia Houses; 9 House of Lead; 10 Makrilithari

terrace on which the House of Shields was built. This tomb was never finished and the cutting must have been abandoned by the beginning of LH IIIB when the terrace for the structure above was completed, possibly because of the imposition of a new restriction. It seems possible that the chamber tomb by Grave Circle B may have belonged to a lesser member of the clan for whom the adjacent Tholos of Clytemnestra was built shortly before the beginning of LH IIIB.

In the Pezoulia area on the north-west slope two apparently commercial establishments from the early part of the period have been discovered. Both were destroyed by fire at the end of the fourteenth century. The southern, the House of the Wine Merchant, had been almost completely obliterated during the construction of a new terraced building in the next period. However, remains of large pithoi in their settings and more than 50 transport stirrup jars accompanied by a handsome rhyton which, being damaged at the point, was then put to mundane use. These stirrup jars, in contrast with those of slightly later date from the House of the Oil Merchant, appeared very clean, thus giving rise to the contrasting name of the building. Slightly further north is another complex known as Petsas' House. Excavation took place here in 1950-1 and restarted in 2000. The remains consist of at least two levels of construction, the upper on the east containing several ground floor rooms and to the west two parallel rows of basement rooms, most of which were used as storerooms for new (unused) vases, originally as many as 500 arranged on shelves by shape and size. The main entrance was located at the south-west corner of the structure and consisted of a narrow ramp of poros slabs leading to an enclosed area for loading/unloading. Here an intriguing group of figurines and unpainted drinking vessels was found. From this area a wide stone staircase ascended by four steps from the basement level to the ground floor. The fill on the stairs and elsewhere in the complex shows the burnt destruction clearly. The fire caused the accidental baking of a partial tablet inscribed in the Linear B script recording the delivery of a product – possibly wool though this is not completely clear. This is the earliest Linear B tablet known so far on the mainland of Greece (**61**).

Remains of other buildings of this phase have been found under those of the early thirteenth century. We can tell little of their architecture but many if not all were decorated with wall paintings (**colour plate 10**).

The structures of the main palatial building period in the early thirteenth century are much more solidly built. It may be suggested that this was meant as a precaution against earthquake damage but it may merely have been intended to make better use of the sloping hillsides. Whatever the reason, the structures, both commercial and private, are constructed on terraces supported by heavy walls on the down slope and filled with stone, earth and sherdage. There are often cross walls within the terraces for extra support and considerable care is taken so that groundwater runs off safely through drains and does not build up within the terrace. The buildings themselves are of two basic types: a long thin corridor plan following the line of a terrace along the hillside, often on two levels, and, where the underlying ground was suitable, a squarer version with rooms arranged around a central area or court. Our French colleagues distinguish between the simpler houses and the more elaborate which they term 'intermediate', i.e. combining features of both palaces and houses. Of these buildings some suffered in the earthquake in the second half of the thirteenth century and went out of use at that time; others continued until the disaster at the end of the century.

Two apparently commercial versions of the long thin type, identified as workshops but not yet published, were found when the foundations of the new site museum were being dug. One has been left open and can be seen on the west of the museum. Another possibly commercial establishment was excavated in 1952 near the Perseia spring and the clay beds at Longaki. A field with plentiful Mycenaean sherds was tested and remains of a house were found. Here the pottery was all of a rather soft clay – probably from these beds without mixing – and of a much poorer quality than usual.

Two of the excavated groups, one simple, one intermediate, of the thirteenth century lie on either side of the modern road south of the Tomb of Clytemnestra and can be easily seen by the visitor (**25**). The 'Ivory Houses' (also called the West House Group or House of the Oil Merchant Group) demonstrate clearly the mixed functions of the intermediate examples. The presence of Linear B tablets in each of the four structures (**61**) indicates a relation to the government bureaucracy. The first to be built were the House of Shields and the West House. The former at the north has a unique plan of two rooms side by side with another across the front at the north. This was a depot where high status items in exotic materials were stored before distribution (**colour plate 11**). The West House was the headquarters. In plan it had a simple megaron arrangement with forecourt and a side passage beside which lay storerooms and a kitchen. It was a house in which people lived but from which personnel working more widely were organised. This we know both from the tablets found in it and from the large (69 examples) collection of small stirrup jars from room 1, for they were used and individually distinct as if they had been left for filling with one of the commodities issued as rations to workers. We now know that such small stirrup jars could contain wine (p.113) and wine is one of the rations listed on the tablets from the West House. There is a problem however: though only 17 people are named in the tablets, the rations seem to be for very large numbers, more even than the 69 of the stirrup jars.

The House of the Oil Merchant downslope to the east lies on two heavy terraces to the west of and beside the main ancient roadway to the citadel from the south. The basement level at the east was well preserved; from here came the material from which the house is named: a room containing 11 pithoi with a catch pit in the middle of the floor and under one of the jars a means of heating the contents as well as a single Linear B tablet (**58** left). Outside the door at the north end of the corridor was found a group of 30 transport stirrup jars almost all from Crete (both west and central). Two of these jars appear oily even today though, as they have been for many years completely restored, they have not been subjected to contents analysis. A surprising fact is that these are the only oily jars known at present so we may speculate whether it is some kind of special oil or actually something fatty rather than oily which has created this appearance. The upper terrace to the west would have supported an upper storey which lay over the extent of both terraces. The fourth house of the group, the House of Sphinxes, is preserved only on the basement level which was given over to storage but here the plan is different. A central corridor is flanked by one room and an open area on the east and three large rooms and a probable stair with cupboard below on the west. In room 1 (on the east) was a unique collection of unused pottery carefully arranged by type and shape with some pots obviously fallen from shelves. In the sill area of the doorway of this room (in very black carbonised earth) were seven sealings with the impression of a man between two goats and inscriptions on the back in the Linear B script listing pots (**60**). Contrary to my first impression when I discovered these, they are now thought not to have sealed the door but to have accompanied incoming goods – here a pottery shipment. This building also served as an assembly point for inlaid furniture: into rooms 2 and 4 had fallen from above large quantities of ivory and wood as well as pumice for polishing the finished pieces.

This group contrasts most interestingly with the group of simpler houses (the Panagia Houses) immediately north of the Treasury of Atreus which can also be taken as typical of the other type of basic house plan. Their very ordinariness is shown by the fact that there was little preserved on their floors despite the obvious destruction from earthquake evidenced by the skeleton of a woman found in one of the doorways.

The long corridor/terrace plan of the Ivory Houses was however used for ordinary houses on the slopes to the north of the citadel, one of which, the Plakes House, was excavated in the 1970s. It was decorated, as were all Mycenaean structures (possibly even storerooms and workshops) with figured wall plaster but in this case the style is as yet unparalleled. This house was damaged in the earthquake in the second half of the thirteenth century when three adults and a child died in the collapse of the basement. In the immediate aftermath a heavy pile of stones was used to support the west terrace wall.

This type of plan also occurs in a structure (or pair of structures) where the function is far from clear. This lies at the extreme south end of the Panagia Ridge and was labelled as a gate by Steffen. The remains were carefully cleared in 1992 during the Mycenae Survey. This showed the plan but no traces of the contents remained on the heavily eroded site. Two long terrace-like buildings are divided by a central area (possibly a roadway) some 6m wide. It is remotely possible that they are houses or some kind of commercial complex (there is a resemblance to the Artisans' Quarter within the citadel) but an elaborate entry is perhaps more likely. The difficulty with this last suggestion, however, is that it is quite clear that the ancient main road did not run along the top of the ridge and therefore an entry or check point here would be unlikely. The road in fact runs lower along the slope to the east where a 'blockhouse' or guardpost has been identified.

South of the Treasury of Atreus there are chamber tombs, several of them very large and well made (this is excellent rock for the purpose) on the lower slopes of the ridge on both east and west but not on the top which is crowned by a series of structures as far at least as the House of Lead which stood on a strong and extensive terrace (20m x 30m in size). Unfortunately only a basement storeroom remained with several pottery vessels and the large lead vat from which the house is named.

Several of the other structures which have been cleared or discovered by chance had been reused as foundations for buildings of the Hellenistic town. This is true of two small square buildings just west of the far entrance to the modern car park and another lying close to the east face of the rock outcrop just below this (**25**). Other areas referred to as houses have been identified by the find of heavy sherd scatters which when investigated produced some walling and groups of pots. Unfortunately such find spots can easily become lost without very accurate surveying. Lisa's House on the slope to the east of the Epano Phournos tholos tomb was tested in 1939 and produced some 'good examples of domestic ware'. The site has been tentatively re-identified by the survey team but no surface traces remain. Further round the slope of the hill, however, the trench where a pottery cupboard was discovered to the south-west of the Cyclopean Terrace Building can still be found and has now been accurately plotted.

As yet unexcavated but with intriguing ground plans visible on the surface are the two large and heavily built structures beside two of the roads (**25**) that lead north from the town. These have been called 'Mansions' though at present we can only speculate as to their function. Some sort of economic control point might be suggested. The last of the fully excavated or partially cleared buildings within the area of what can be called Greater Mycenae is the farmhouse at Khania. This lies just to the south of the circular burial platform (below p.140) and can be visited (**3**). This was excavated in the late 1980s but has not been published. Features that have been reported include storage rooms with pithoi and an entry ramp (like that excavated at Gla) to enable agricultural produce to be brought into the building easily. This building is of particular importance as no other building apparently of this type has been found at any site. Its position on the direct route from the citadel of Mycenae to Argos – adjacent to the site of the Ottoman Han from which the area takes its name – suggests that it might have had a mixed function as rural site and stopping point on an important route.

Tombs

The first major construction of this phase is probably the so-called Treasury of Atreus (Tomb of Agamemnon in Greek though neither name has any historic validity whatsoever). There is argument, very difficult to resolve, as to its date of construction: the end of LH IIIA1 on the basis of the pottery from an extensive refuse deposit sealed by the rock chips from cutting the tomb, or LH IIIB mid on the basis of a single sherd found under the threshold. On balance it seems more likely that the single sherd is an intrusion from refurbishment of the doorway for later usage.

This tomb is the most striking monument at Mycenae today and in antiquity would have been even more striking with its two colour façade (**26**) and the handsome enclosure wall around the dome in cut poros stone. There is very considerable architectural advance between the last tholos of the previous period

26 *The façade of the Treasury of Atreus: the fill of the relieving triangle is of bands of red stone and the columns are of green stone, both probably from the Argolid.* © Mycenae Archive: Charles K. Williams II

(the Lion Tomb beside the site museum) and the Treasury of Atreus. Its overall size, the size of the blocks used, and the elaboration of the façade and enclosure wall distinguish it clearly.

The last tholos of the nine to be constructed was the Tomb of Clytemnestra, raided by Veli Pasha and excavated first by Mrs Schliemann. It is usually dated to the end of the fourteenth century. A notable advance in building was the wider use of sawn conglomerate, but this proved detrimental to its stability as faults in the blocks did not come to light during manufacture, only in time. The façade of this tomb too was decorated by this time by half columns of gypsum with vertical fluting – which may possibly have been the means by which fluting, common on ephemeral Mycenaean wooden and ivory columns (**27**), was passed to builders of the first millennium.

At one time it was suggested on the basis of the material (no gypsum was used in the Treasury of Atreus) that the sculptures in gypsum from the Elgin collection in

27 *Miniature columns in ivory from the House of Shields, thirteenth century BC (53-436 NM 7429 & 53-437 NM 7430; life-size).*
© Mycenae Archive:
T. Leslie Shear Jnr

the British Museum might have come from this tomb but this is impossible. The blocks reached the British Museum well before the tomb could have been looted by Veli Pasha. On the east side at least the mound over the top of the tomb was enclosed by a wall, of well-cut poros blocks at the south end and less impressive at the north. Against these lay several unusual deposits of pottery – apparently dedications – and it is from the earliest of these that we can suggest a date for the completion of the tomb.

The third tomb of the last group, the Tomb of the Genii (after the motifs on glass plaques found in it, though sometimes called the Perfect Tomb) is harder to date. In many of its constructional details it resembles the Treasury of Atreus of which in general it seems to be a smaller version though there are also parallels to others of the series. There were three grave pits in the floor but the whole tomb had been robbed leaving only an assortment of small ornaments and jewellery scattered around. It is likely that this tomb comes between the former two and dates from the second half of the fourteenth century.

The tholos was the tomb for the highest social group. Others used family chamber tombs: rooms or caves cut into the soft rock (often under a hard ledge) approached by an open passageway or dromos. It was originally suggested by Wace that the large well-cut tombs were later than the smaller ones with short wide dromoi sloping down sharply. The work of Dr Shelton on the chamber tomb cemeteries at Mycenae has shown that almost all were cut in the Early Palatial period and therefore the differences in size and type should be assigned to status as well as to the quality of the rock in the areas chosen. At present there are 27 known cemeteries (**10**) but new tombs are discovered even now in these and other cemeteries will certainly come to light. The total of chamber tombs known in the Mycenae area now approaches 300.

The work of the Mycenae Survey as well as marking the location of these tombs (almost all of which had come to light *after* Steffen made his maps) has enabled us to disprove one theory of Tsountas and his successors and to support another. We now know that the distinct arrangement of cemeteries does not reflect a series of small settlements surrounding the citadel. There are absolutely no signs of structures in almost all cases particularly none near the many cemeteries to the north of the site. Tsountas had noted the structures on the Panagia ridge above three of the cemeteries

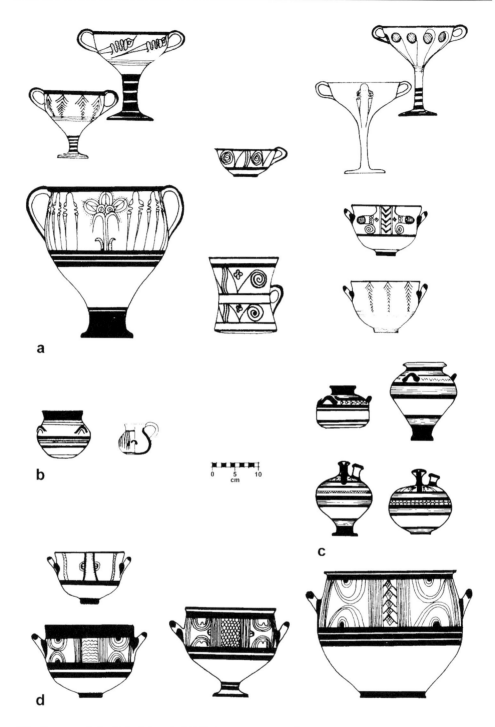

28   *Pottery of the Palatial period LH IIIA2 – IIIB.* © Mycenae Archive.
   a. Stage 4: drinking vessels and a krater LH IIIA 2 (left) and LH IIIB1 (right);
   b. Stage 4: LH IIIB1 cult vessels; c. Stage 4: LH IIIB1 export vessels;
   d. Stage 5: LH IIIB2 open vessels

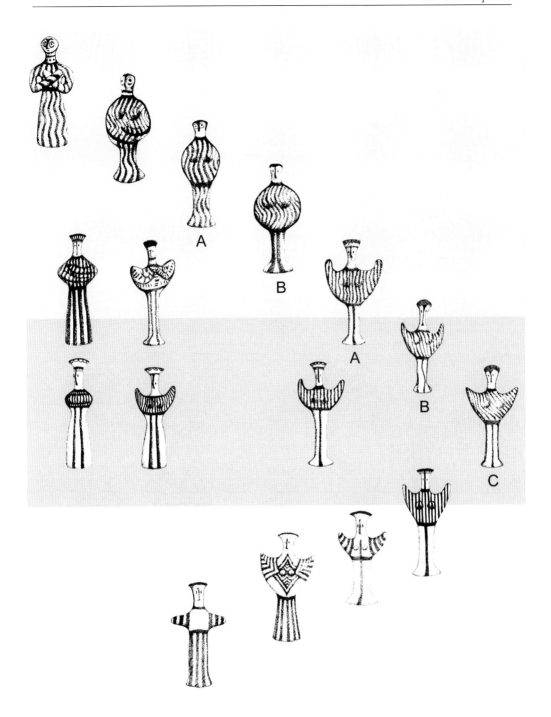

29 *The development and types of female figurines. Not to scale. A typical figurine stands about 5in (12cm) tall. The darker shading indicates the thirteenth century BC.*
© Tamara McNicol 1974 amended Sibby Postgate 2001

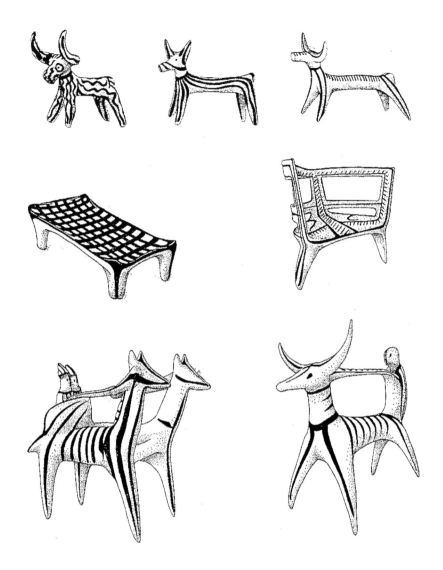

30 Terracotta figurines, type examples of animals (with Wavy, Linear and Spine decora-
tion) (©Tamara McNicol) and groups (Bed or Bier, Lattice Throne, Chariot and
Plough group). Not to scale. © Mycenae Archive

and Wace took as supporting evidence the structures, which are in fact largely of
earlier periods, on the Kalkani hill. We would now suggest that the location of the
cemeteries reflects some form of land holding of families or clans. On the other hand
Tsountas' suggestion that the position of the cemeteries might be related to the road
system seems likely. We cannot, however, tell which comes first. Are the cemeteries
placed near the roads or are the roads positioned to serve the cemeteries? Perhaps the
truth is a combination of both factors.

An additional factor seems to be related: the presence, adjacent to some of the cemeteries, of resources such as clay or stone. It seems unlikely that the cemeteries belong to the actual workers in these materials but the clay pit or quarry may have belonged to the family whose cemetery lay nearby. In this case the roads would have facilitated exploitation.

Occasional burials of other types occur throughout this period and there are scattered skeletal remains like those in the well found below the Cyclopean Terrace Building. But, though this has often been debated, it seems unlikely that at Mycenae itself any class of the population was buried in any other way than in a chamber tomb. It is, however, very hard to estimate how many people were buried in the chamber tombs (let alone the tholoi all of which had been robbed) as the basic burial custom allowed both the remains of the dead and the offerings placed with them to be swept to one side when the tomb was opened for reuse. It seems likely that once the flesh had gone, the remains did not require veneration or care. The occasional traces of burning found in chamber tombs are thought to result from a form of fumigation which would have been necessary if the tomb had to be reopened soon after one burial to make way for another.

The grave goods found in chamber tombs become less costly through time. By the Palatial period they consisted mainly of pottery (**28**) and some personal adornment (**colour plate 8** bottom) with an occasional exotic item. The pottery was mainly storage vessels which had probably contained oils or unguents (cf **28c**). Fragments of kylikes (**54**) are often found around the doorway of the tomb and have been interpreted as part of a farewell ritual of libation or toasting. They may be accompanied by animal bones from feasting of some kind. The jewellery is of semi-precious stone or of glass. Some burials are accompanied by small terracotta figurines, female, animal and group pieces (**29 & 30**), the significance of which is still uncertain, though they may on occasion indicate a child burial. In the early part of the period (the fourteenth century) some imported items were deposited, notably stone vessels from Egypt or Canaanite amphorai from the Levant (**50**), but even this seems to die out by the thirteenth century. It is likely that this restriction of burial ostentation results from sumptuary control by the palace though it is unclear whether it was for social or economic reasons.

7 The excavated structures within the citadel

[See plan **19** throughout]

The Lion Gate (1) (**front cover**) was built about the middle of the thirteenth century BC as a new main entrance to the citadel. With the triangular limestone relief over the lintel it forms one of the most imposing structures of all time. The gate was heavily obscured by fallen debris, possibly completely (see p.19), until the early nineteenth century. It was finally cleared in 1841 by Pittakes for the Archaeological Society and the two blocks on the right of the relief were replaced in position by the Anastylosis Service in 1950.

The approach followed a natural uphill path from the north and led to a forecourt between the smooth, steep rock on the left topped by a new handsome facing wall in front of the old fortification and a sturdy bastion on the right, the unprotected side of a warrior carrying a shield on his left.

The gate itself consists of four single blocks of conglomerate: the lintel and threshold each weigh over 20 tons; the two jambs are smaller. These enormous blocks, like the stones that were used in the construction of the wall, were rolled into place on ramps and the finishing was carried out on the spot.

The threshold shows several cuttings. There are three, slightly irregular grooves, which were once thought to have been ruts from chariot wheels, but which were in fact cut at a much later date to assist the drainage of rainwater from the inner part of the gate. It is also covered with shallow cuttings to prevent animals from slipping; there is a shallow square hole in the middle of the front edge and a smaller, circular hole further in. These cuttings too were all made later; they belong to the Archaic or perhaps even to the Hellenistic period. The only Mycenaean features are two cuttings at the inner angles of the jambs, originally round in shape, but later worn or altered; there are two corresponding cylindrical holes in the lintel. These accommodated the pivots for the doors: two rounded vertical beams with protruding ends which rotated within the holes as the leaves of the door opened or shut. The door jambs have a projecting ledge at the outside, about 4in (0.1m) deep, which continues along the length of the lintel; this formed a frame that stopped the leaves of the door from swivelling outwards. On the inner face of the jambs there are two square holes; into these fitted the ends of a square wooden beam which could keep the door securely shut. Other oblong holes, two on each jamb, were probably intended to fit the handles of the doors so that they could be pushed wide open.

In order to relieve the lintel of some of the weight of the superstructure, the ashlar courses above either end, resting on the door jambs, corbel out progressively, leaving a triangular empty space – a so-called relieving triangle, characteristic of Mycenaean architecture. For practical as well as aesthetic reasons, this empty triangle was filled with a slab of hard limestone bearing in relief two lions after which the gate is named. This is the earliest example of monumental sculpture known in Europe. The lions stand heraldically on their hind legs, facing each other, with their front paws on two small altars. Their heads, which were apparently shown frontally, have not survived; the size of the dowel holes on the slab indicate that they were made of some heavy material, possibly steatite. Standing on the small altars between the lions, there is a column that supports the entablature of a building. This shows that the column was not meant to represent a deity (as was once suggested) but symbolises a building, most probably the palace itself, the royal house of Mycenae, of which the lions are both guardians and symbols. Both the carving and the composition of the relief echo signet rings of an earlier period from which the pose may be thought to have been copied.

Beyond the gate there is a small square courtyard which was originally roofed; it is flanked on the right by a free-standing wall beyond which was a stair giving access to the roofed space and presumably also to the fortification wall itself; on the left the court is flanked by the rock, masked by a conglomerate facing. This facing is broken by a small space, which was once thought to have been used by the guard or to have housed a watch-dog, but the suggestion (made originally by Charitonides) that it was a gate shrine is now, though impossible of proof, widely accepted. There are similar features both in the North Gate at Mycenae and on other sites, notably at Gla where there are also proper guardrooms at each of the gates.

The Granary (2) takes its name from the plant remains (carbonised wheat, barley and vetches in vessels of both baked and unbaked clay) found in, and fallen into, its basements, though it is perhaps best known for the pottery style of LH IIIC Middle named after it. The original excavation by Schliemann was completed by Wace but many problems remain, not least of which is the intended function of the building.

The façade was clearly planned in relation to Grave Circle A, thus showing that it was built later than the circle. The walls are founded on the rock but the floors lie on an earth and stone terrace fill; as so often it is the basement level which survives though there is good evidence of the level above from which the building was entered. The basement was reached from this level by a well-built staircase (of which the bottom two steps survive). Windows in the west and south face gave some light to these basements.

On the north-east side of the building – facing the courtyard of the Lion Gate – there are two narrow parallel corridors leading to an entry, probably belonging to the second and third stage of the building's history; they themselves were later extended on a slightly different axis. Thus the building has at least three, possibly four, building phases and indeed thanks to its very solid construction was kept in use until a major destruction that foreshadowed the final collapse of the citadel.

The fact that the terrace on which the Granary stands abuts against the citadel wall and that there is no passage along the wall at this point has been taken as an indication that it was built after the devastation of 1200 BC. This is confirmed by the fact that the entry level lay at the height of the debris covering the stair by the Lion Gate.

The pottery found in the Granary and particularly in the two basements, and, generally speaking, the class to which it belongs is known as the Granary Class, comprising monochrome painted and rough plain wares. Many fragments of the elaborate miniature Close Style (**67**), which exemplifies a last floruit of Mycenaean civilization, were found in the fill of the basements and are usually associated with the pottery from the destruction levels. A bath grave with pottery offerings of the final phase was found above the debris from the destruction of the Granary in the area of the Lion Gate staircase.

Grave Circle A (3) (section **8**) is now recognised as a group of high status burials which were specially respected within the larger contemporary cemetery and later enclosed within the walls as a unique monument. No building ever took place over the circle and a unique inscribed sherd of about 475 BC saying 'To the hero' came from the overlying debris suggesting that the area may have been considered special even in later times.

This was the area first and notably excavated by Schliemann and the finds form the core display of the Mycenaean Room in the National Museum in Athens (**colour plate 7**). It was restudied in detail and fully published by Karo. The whole area has been heavily restored and few original details are now obvious.

Originally – i.e. in the sixteenth century BC – a group of large shaft graves, unquestionably used for 'royal' burials, were dug on the slope in the centre of the 'Prehistoric Cemetery', and were demarcated by a low circular rubble wall at the west of which only a very small section has remained. Later in the mid–thirteenth century when the fortifications were to be extended it was realised that the natural line of the new west wall would have run along the rock ridge immediately east of these graves, so the wall was taken in a curve further west. Indeed even the line then planned seems to have had to be slightly altered as the line of the wall as built shows clearly. This may have been because the graves would otherwise have been relegated to the bottom of a large, artificial hollow, practically inaccessible and possibly dangerous, owing to the water that would gather there. In order to bring the burial ground to the level of the acropolis entrance, a stout wall with distinct inward batter was built on the slope over the old enclosure, to retain the fill covering the graves and the fortification wall was adjusted to make room for this. The new support wall levelled the ground artificially, and was topped by upright slabs of soft stone – a shelly sandstone – forming two concentric circles, approximately 1m apart. The slabs were of equal height, and the interval between the two circles was roofed by similar, horizontal slabs supported by small wooden beams set in sockets cut in the vertical slabs. Thus the slabs form a circular, apparently compact parapet. Facing almost due north and near the Lion Gate, there is an entrance with three threshold slabs, between the two square cross walls which terminate the circle on either side.

This later enclosure, some 26m in diameter, contained the six large shaft graves, numbered from I to VI, and some seven ordinary graves, small and shallow, which were largely destroyed in the course of the early excavations, as well as a further one, only discovered in 1956, half-covered by the slabs of the parapet. Schliemann excavated five out of the six graves; Stamatakis excavated the sixth grave, nearest to the entrance; the inner row of parapet slabs passes across the angle of this grave. All six were family tombs containing the remains of 18 people: nine men, eight women and one child. At least 11 stelai were erected over the tombs, of which some survived whole and others in fragments (**7**). Because they were moved from their original positions when the later circle, contemporary with the Lion Gate, was built in the thirteenth century BC, it is not possible to ascertain whether the sculptured stelai were destined for the men and the plain ones for the women, as has been suggested.

The Great Ramp (4) lies immediately beyond the area inside the Lion Gate and is, in its present form, part of the same building scheme. The earlier phases belong to the first fortification schemes (**16**). Though it was partially cleared by Schliemann, details of its history were only finally revealed by the work of Mylonas published in 1965.

This is a Cyclopean structure, with a low parapet on the west and a 1:5 slope, i.e. suitable only for those on foot or for pack animals. A Mycenaean wall of mudbrick with timber framing edged the east side but is now covered by a Hellenistic wall of ashlar masonry. A large drain to take away water from the top was constructed within the structure with an outlet to the south of Grave Circle A. The Ramp stops abruptly at the south end where the route to the top of the acropolis must have turned sharply to the east.

The latest ramp runs in the opposite direction to the original one and had an earlier phase itself when it was both much narrower and less steep, thus allowing a passage leading south along the east side of the Grave Circle. However, the ramp was later broadened until the foundations encroached on one or two slabs of the Grave Circle parapet, and the passage became obstructed.

The Little Ramp (5) (**31**) is a neglected and misunderstood feature. It lies immediately above and to the east of the Ramp House but has no apparent function after the Great Ramp was widened in the last stage of the major development of the citadel; at this point the Little Ramp was blocked off at the north and probably used as further strengthening of the terrace to the east after the earthquake. Originally it could be approached by the path between Grave Circle A and the Great Ramp and led to the terrace immediately above and to the east of the Cult Centre. We know that there was a major structure here with conglomerate thresholds and column bases but this terrace has never been excavated. Access to this upper terrace was gained in the last phase by a steep twisting path leading from the poros causeway (see below). It is from this upper terrace that the inscribed tablets found fallen into the corridor at the east of the Cult Centre must have originated.

The Ramp House (6) (**31**) is one of three houses in the sector to the south of Grave Circle A opening onto a small open space. At the time of building both the

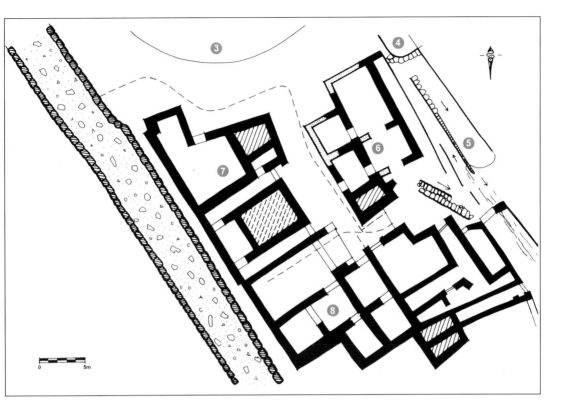

31 *Houses south of Grave Circle A.* © Mycenae Archive.
    3. Grave circle A; 4. Great Ramp; 5. Little Ramp; 6. Ramp House; 7. House of the
    Warrior Vase; 8. South House with its annex on the east

Ramp House and the South House would have been reached easily from the west but after the construction of the Grave Circle and the fortification wall the approaches would have been more restricted: along inside the fortification wall and up the path by the House of the Warrior Vase or rather deviously from above by the Processional Way.

The Ramp House lies on the upper east rock level and is supported by a strong terrace wall along the rock ledge. The remains of the latest period, where two building phases can be identified, overlie at least two other earlier buildings as well as graves of the Prehistoric Cemetery. Within the terrace below the megaron and the east corridor as well as outside the building to the north came an important group of fresco fragments showing a bull leaping scene recently restudied by Dr Maria Shaw (*BSA* 91). It has generally been supposed that these originated in a building somewhere on the slope above to the east – for the Palace, as suggested once by Evans, is too far away. But Dr Shaw suggests, in the light of recent work on the Cult Centre to the south, that the earlier building below the Ramp House itself may be the source.

The plan of the later building, which probably dates to the early years of the thirteenth century, seems to share features with two of the more recently excavated houses outside the walls. In the West House the megaron faces south and has a row of ancillary rooms off a corridor to the west but in the House of the Oil Merchant the ancillary rooms form a basement level within the terrace structure – because of the slope of the rock. The Ramp House is similar. One of the basement rooms could be entered directly from the west and that at the north was probably approached from this room. The corner 'room' at the south-west, however, like the 'corridor' at the east, seems to have been a structural feature strengthening the terrace on which the house was built.

The House Of The Warrior Vase (7) (**31**) was excavated by Schliemann who thought it was Agamemnon's palace. Because it was excavated so early and has now been very drastically restored, much of the interpretation is problematic (see also p.140 below). The remains appear to be those of another house with heavy basements, two of which can be entered directly from outside but with a main entrance on an upper floor at the level of the entrances to the other two adjacent houses. It is quite clear that it was planned after the new Grave Circle and it abuts against the South House. On the other hand the drain which runs under the approach passage toward the basements and on to the fortification wall is clearly laid out to avoid it as well as other pre-existing features. It may therefore be suggested that the House of the Warrior Vase was laid out as part of a single development plan with Grave Circle A and the fortification wall.

The layout suggests that there might have been a megaron facing west over the southern room but this would have faced directly into the fortification wall and the alignment may therefore have been quite different. The arrangement of rooms is less canonical than that of the earlier Ramp House but has echoes of the later South House Annex. Once again the corner space without a door may have had a structural function only. An interesting feature is the north-west corner which is indented to avoid a well, though another probable well was abandoned when the east wall of the south-east room was built.

Among Schliemann's finds (which may have originated in the house itself if it continued in use after the devastation of 1200 BC or in the wash above it or even be associated with a later burial) were not only the fragments of the large late Mycenaean krater (**colour plate 19**) decorated with the figures of warriors after which the building is named, but also a handsome Naue type sword (**51**) and two large bronze vessels, one a tripod. Underlying the house were several graves of the Prehistoric Cemetery.

The South House (8) (**31**) is the largest and probably the earliest major building on this lower terrace and it is at a quite different orientation from the cult buildings immediately to the south. The house with its annex comprises three sets of rooms; a larger group at the west forms the South House proper (excavated by Schliemann 1876, then Wace 1920, Taylour 1954-69 and finally Mylonas) with two groups to the east forming the South House Annex (excavated by Taylour). The main section has been consolidated and conservation of the Annex which was built partly of

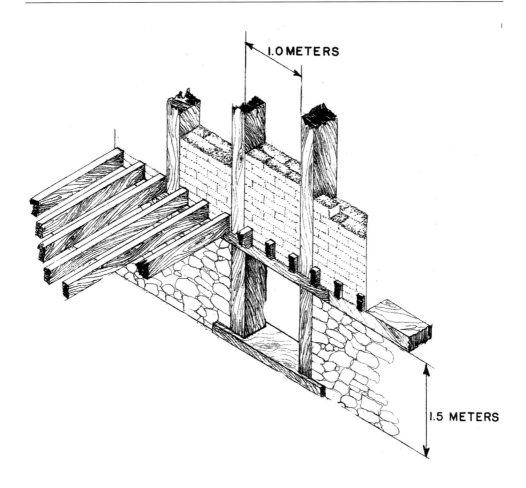

1.0 METERS

1.5 METERS

32 *Mycenaean construction technique: stone foundation with upper wall of mudbrick and*
timber ties, based on evidence from the House of Sphinxes.
© Mycenae Archive: Charles K. William II

mudbrick on stone socles rather than a whole foundation storey of stone, was initiated in 1998-9.

The house itself stands on a massive free-standing terrace from the fill of which clear evidence for a construction date early in the thirteenth century BC has been obtained – one of our few really tangible pieces of evidence. The entry lay at the north-east corner from the open space in front of the Ramp House over a handsome threshold into a long room from which three others, almost square, are entered. Beyond the eastern two of these two further rooms can be reached. The walls of the ground floor are of stone and have the recesses for the vertical and horizontal timbering by which the upper storey of mudbrick was stabilised (**32**). A stairway of cist slabs seems to have led to the upper storey and evidence for the construction of the ceilings and floors was also recovered.

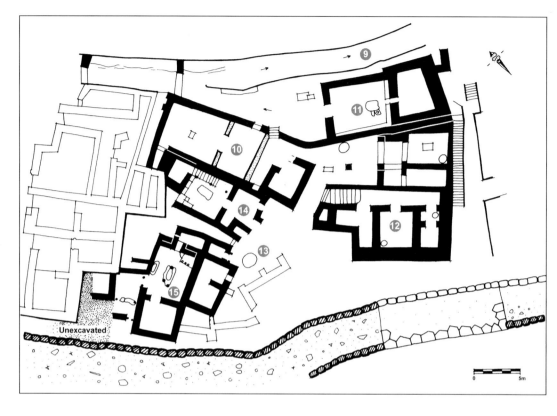

33 Cult Centre. © Mycenae Archive.
9. Processional Way; 10. Megaron; 11. Shrine Gamma; 12. Tsountas' House;
13. Central Court; 14. Temple; 15. Room with the Fresco Complex

The Annex has three separate entrances again from the space in front of the Ramp House leading to two independent sections. Immediately east of the main structure there is the entry to a basement which may have been separate (like that of the Ramp House) or opened to the south to stairs. Further east at a higher level an entrance leads into a series of corridors and small storage rooms from which access would have been possible to a larger room over the basement. At a higher level still and forming the easternmost section of the Annex was a storeroom with emplacements for large vats and amphorae including an imported one of the Canaanite type (**50**).

The small courtyard which divides the South House Annex from the Ramp House is crossed by a series of drains which join up with those leading out both directly to the fortification wall and along under the approach passage from the north. Its most notable feature however is a rock cut causeway edged by poros blocks which leads from the Ramp House to a roofed corridor that connects this part of the site with the Processional Way and the Cult Centre to the south.

The Cult Centre (9-15) (**33**) comprises a group of five complex structures and was identified as such by Mylonas. Two of the buildings were originally excavated by

Tsountas and thus are named for him; the others came to light in the last seasons of work by Lord William Taylour. The whole area has since been comprehensively investigated by Mylonas. The finds from the Cult Centre are some of the most intriguing to be found at Mycenae in recent years and form a focal point of the display in the site museum.

Though the area of the Cult Centre lies immediately south of the South House and its Annex, on the west it lies at a considerably lower level and the northern part faces in the opposite direction at a slightly different angle.

These various buildings were built in apparent succession from the end of the fourteenth century BC to the middle of the thirteenth, all it would seem before the construction of the fortification wall. Shortly after the last of them was completed, some kind of disaster overtook the area followed by extensive restoration and alteration. Some buildings remained in use after this until a great fire at the end of the century. This devastation filled the whole area with debris and reoccupation took place only at a much higher level.

The area could be approached in three ways: from the upper slopes of the citadel (i.e. the Grand Staircase of the palace area) by the Processional Way, from the north by a roofed and plastered corridor that runs to the east of the South House Annex (continuing from the poros causeway that starts in front of the Ramp House) and from the west through an open court. As the structures appear to have been built before the citadel wall, the court would have been open to the west. Later it could only have been approached from both north and south by passages along the inside of the fortification wall.

The furthermost section of the *Processional Way* (9) to have been excavated runs at a gentle incline from north to south. After a flight of 14 poros steps and a landing it turns back on itself and runs north. This section of the Processional Way was roofed and the wall running along the slope was coated with plaster which retained fresco decoration in situ: marbling and a chariot scene facing left, i.e. north toward the Cult Centre. Beyond this was a threshold with the circular cuttings for doorposts at either end, indicating that the passage could be closed off at this point by double doors. From here the passage slopes down towards the south end of the corridor by the South House Annex. Here it again doubles back and slopes down past the entrance to the Megaron to a small court leading directly into the Shrine exposed first by Tsountas.

The Megaron (10), which is named from its restored plan, is entered from the last section of the Processional Way over a well cut threshold of laminated limestone with a handsome anta block preserved beside it. At this point the floor of the main level has collapsed into a series of basement rooms. Over these an anteroom is restored leading to a large room at the north which was built on a heavy terrace. In the centre was a square hearth. There seems to have been an exit at the north-west corner leading to storage rooms at a lower level. The copious contents of the basements (pottery, scrap ivory, boar's tusks, glass jewellery etc) compares with the material found in other areas of the Cult Centre. At least two building stages were identified before the building was destroyed by a devastating fire.

34 *Temple in the Cult Centre from the south.* © Mycenae Archive: W.D. Taylour

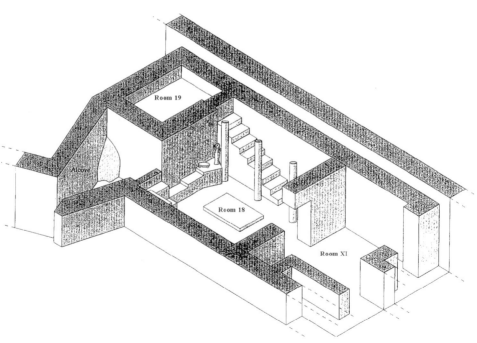

35 *Isometric view of the Temple in the Cult Centre.* © Mycenae Archive: prepared by Ben Wilmore from an original drawing by Martin Goalen

South of the Megaron a flight of five poros steps led to a passage that may have served as a means of access to the upper levels of the Temple to the west.

Shrine Gamma (11) is the higher of two buildings lying on a terraced slope excavated by Tsountas. This was the earlier to be built and had a clear cult function. The plan is rectangular, oriented roughly north to south, and consisting of two rooms, one opening into the other behind. In the northern larger room, in which two phases of use were clear, were a horseshoe shaped plaster altar with an installation for libation offerings and a large unworked stone sunk into the floor in the room's centre. The purpose of this is unclear. The rear room is small and square with no obvious floor above the uncut rock; it has been interpreted as the *adyton* or inner sanctuary from the stray cult items found in it but from its plan and position it may originally have been another corner tower as in the houses of similar date.

In the open area just outside the building and immediately to the left of the entrance was another altar apparently made of a stone slab base and an upper portion which has not been preserved whether it was of stone, wood or other ephemeral material. In front of the altar was a low platform or step of plaster. This is the spot to which the 'Processional Way' led from higher on the slope.

Tsountas' House (12), the second building at the south of the complex, was built downslope from and after Shrine Gamma; it is more likely to have had a domestic function. The house lies on two levels built on adjacent terraces from east to west. On the upper level is a typical megaron with the addition of two small rooms along the west side, while on the lower terrace is a basement of three rectangular rooms opening onto a corridor and reached by a stone staircase from the terrace above. There was originally an upper storey of unknown plan above the basements. The house has been interpreted as a residence for those conducting cult activities.

The Central Court (13) lies on the lower terrace beside the basement level of Tsountas' House; it consists of a forecourt in which stood a round altar of clay mixed with small stones and on the south-west side a shallow stoa roofed by thin slabs of schist. To the west was found a pit with remains of offerings. Building remains beside the altar remain problematic awaiting full publication. The whole area of the court was covered by a thick layer of plesia-like wash, covered in its turn by deep levels of later reoccupation and wash.

The Temple (14) (**34 & 35**) also lay at the intermediate level facing the central court. It is so-called because it is a 'free-standing building of cult purpose'. It was entered from the south through an anteroom equipped with various features (a hearth, a basin and a bench). Immediately west of the entry was an alcove which seems to have been the start of a stair to the upper floor, thus linking with the passage from the poros steps. The main room had three wooden columns along the east side, a central platform (there was no sign of burning) and a series of small platforms or benches along the north side. Marks on the east wall may show where the rough plaster wall was covered by a textile suspended from a wooden slat. At the east end of the low platforms were displayed in situ a red painted terracotta figure and a small portable altar (**36**). Rising from the north-east corner was a stair, which probably originally connected up to the Megaron; the landing was later

36 Bench at the north end of
    the Temple in the Cult
    Centre with figure and
    small clay altar in situ.
    © Mycenae Archive:
    W.D. Taylour

37 Terracotta figure of type A from
    the sealed storeroom behind the
    Temple (68-1577 MM 28975;
    height 11.5in, 29cm). These
    painted figures probably repre-
    sented a deity. © Mycenae
    Archive: E.B. French

38 Terracotta figure of type B from the sealed
    storeroom behind the Temple (68-1596 MM
    28982; height 21.85in, 55.5cm). These mono-
    chrome figures probably represented worshippers.
    © Mycenae Archive: W.D. Taylour

39 Terracotta figure of a snake from the
    sealed storeroom behind the Temple (68-
    1574 MM 28985, diameter 9.5in,
    24cm). The symbolism of the snake
    figures is problematic.
    © Mycenae Archive: E.B. French

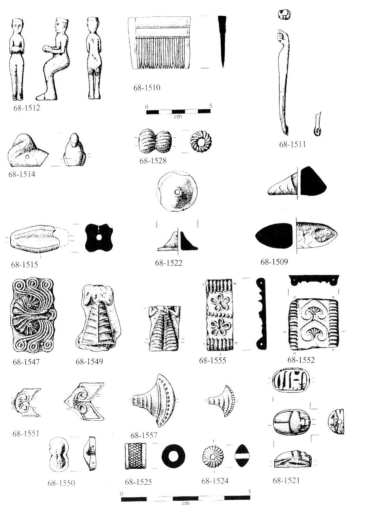

40 Part of the cache of small objects found in a small unpainted bowl (68-1402 MM 16465)
    in the sealed storeroom behind the Temple (the cache numbers 68-1510>1559, MM
    18395>445, though not in the same order). © Mycenae Archive: Michael Lowe.
    Amber: 68-1509; Faience: 68-1515, 1524, 1525, 1528, 1557; Faience scarab of
    Queen Tyi from Egypt: 68-1521; Glass: 68-1547, 1549, 1550, 1551, 1552, 1555;
    Ivory: 68-1510, 1511, 1512; Rock Crystal: 68-1514; Steatite: 68-1522

41 Room with the Fresco and Shrine in the Cult Centre from the west after the removal of the fresco on the east wall of the former. The stone paving on the right marks where the debris with dedications was sealed after being deliberately covered following the earth-quake disaster. © Mycenae Archive: W.D. Taylour

converted into a small storeroom which was found filled with figures and other cult paraphernalia (**37-40**). The door to this room had been sealed with plaster which was then polished. A similar deposit of cult material was found behind the platforms at the north-west corner of the room in an alcove, stacked on a section of naked rock that had originally been visible from within the room, lit by light from a passage to the west. The entry to the whole building is angled so that the line of sight is directed to the figure in situ at the north-east. After the small room was sealed the main room remained in use until being destroyed by the devastating fire which characterised this part of the site.

The *Room with the Fresco* complex (15) lies at a slightly lower level. The central room (**41**) with an elaborate hearth with wooden columns at either end was origi-nally approached from the central court by a passage to the east. In alterations which seem to have occurred very soon after the first construction, entry was moved to the north-west through an anteroom, a small shrine (an inner sanctum where items of significance were also stored) was built at the east and the wall south of the entrance

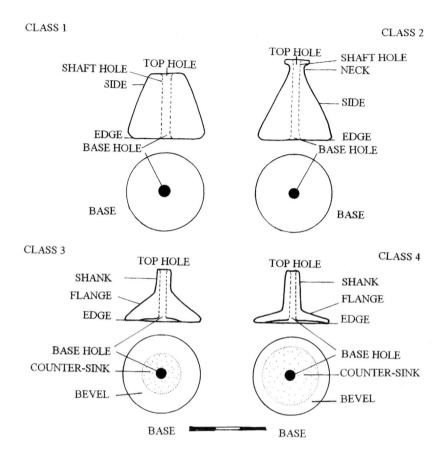

42 *Diagram of the types of Conuli. If these are spindle whorls as is sometimes suggested*
    they would be used the other way up. © Mycenae Archive: Steven Diamant

to the shrine decorated with a fresco (**colour plate 12**) which would have been
visible as one entered the room. Immediately beside the entrance was a clay larnax
which may have served for ritual cleansing. West of the main room lay a square room
in which almost nothing was found; the area of the anteroom and the approach from
the north have not been fully excavated.

In front of the fresco was an altar 60cm high with three small hearths near the
outer edge. On the floor lay a mass of objects, above all pottery of many different
types. Immediately in front of the altar was a group of nine pots, seven for storage
and two for cooking. These have been analysed for their contents (below p.132).
With them was a large lead vessel in which was resting part of an Egyptian plaque
(**colour plate 17**) (some 100 years old at the time the building was destroyed) which
had been carefully split. At the south end of the altar lay tumbled a group of rich
items: a Cretan stone bowl and two handsome ivories (the pommel of a sword and
a couchant lion, **colour plate 14**, originally mounted on a sceptre or on a piece of

furniture). More puzzling was the quantity, found throughout this room and the adjacent one, of small stone conuli (**42**) whose function is still a matter of fierce discussion. A short distance in front of the altar there lay on the floor the ivory head of a presumably male figure (**colour plate 13**). This had probably fallen off the altar where, mounted on a wooden armature or frame draped in cloth, it would have served as a cult object, representing a deity.

Behind (east of) the Room with the Fresco was a small room identified as a shrine or inner sanctum. In the south-west corner was a low dais on which stood one of the smaller figures of type A with, in front of her, what seems to have been an elaborate pectoral decorated with glass 'beehive' beads (**colour plate 18**) and other ornaments. The room also contained much pottery and ivory, both finished objects and stock pieces of partially worked material. Also reached by the passage which ran between the Temple and the Room with the Fresco was, at a higher level, an area, possibly open or only partially roofed, where items very comparable with those from the actual cult rooms were stored. Three further rooms lay to the south of the Room with the Fresco; that at the east seems to have been a small shrine but the other two, which are exceptionally sturdily built, appear to have had an independent function.

The main part of the complex was taken out of use at the time of the 'disaster' and was not used during the last years of the thirteenth century BC though it would have been visible. The fresco was whitewashed and a filling of fine soil was laid over the cult items and dedications. Over this, along the sides of the room where such items were known to lie, a series of large slabs was tidily laid. It seems likely that the decision to 'mothball' this complex may have been taken because access had become so restricted following the construction of the fortification wall.

The Hellenistic Tower (16) stands at the west end of a stone staircase of the Mycenaean period next to an open drain which descends towards the fortification wall from a point just before the conglomerate threshold and doorway in the Processional Way. From this point there would have been access to the upper citadel. Several of those who work at Mycenae think that a west gate lies under the debris against the fortification wall here which has been only partially excavated. This would have been important after the construction of the fortification wall cut off direct access from the west to this part of the citadel. The outer face of the fortification wall was probably destroyed by the Argives and like the section of the wall adjacent to the Lion Gate was repaired in polygonal masonry as a tower during the Hellenistic period.

Against the inner face of the wall by the Hellenistic Tower lay deep strata of the Post-Palatial period. This accumulation resulted from three successive building levels involving several superimposed floors and resulting in a 9.5ft (2.9m) thick deposit, additional evidence for the considerable length of the LH IIIC period. The uppermost layer was topped by the floor and cistern of the Hellenistic structure which crowned the Tower.

The South-west Quarter (17) (**19**) is the name given to the buildings on the lower levels of the west slope of the citadel to the south of Tsountas' House (and the stairway and drain alongside it), within the fortifications of the second phase.

The area was densely occupied by at least 11 houses numbered by the letters Alpha to Lambda of the Greek alphabet. (Some confusion can arise from the fact that Greek letters are also used for buildings in other areas of the acropolis and for excavation sectors e.g. those sectors used by Kritseli-Probidi in her publication of the fresco fragments from this area.) These buildings were first excavated by Tsountas, who left them unpublished and, indeed, unmentioned in his diaries. Practically everywhere Tsountas' excavation reached bedrock but a few pockets and floors were left untouched – enough to justify a fresh investigation by Mylonas (1966-74) and Iakovides (1988-9). Sherds, remnants of walls and a burial under the floor of Zeta 3, showed that the area was inhabited in Middle Helladic times and then abandoned to be occupied again in the thirteenth century by houses. These houses, built on a fairly steep gradient, are divided by straight lanes into two to three successive levels, *c.*4ft (1.25m) wide, and into blocks of five or six houses, separated by stairways built over drains which run downhill toward the Cyclopean wall.

On the upper part of the slope bedrock was high enough to preclude basements. Instead, floors, consisting mainly of a coat of yellow clay mixed with lime, were laid on the rock which showed through in places, or on a fill of earth and rubble of varying thickness as in Beta 1. This room, moreover, virtually the only one left untouched by Tsountas, had benches built along its sides and a rectangular feature in the middle with only faint traces of burning, perhaps an altar rather than a hearth.

Lower down the slope the rooms are obviously basements, communicating with the lanes along their sides but not connected to each other. The lower part of the walls was built of rubble and they had superstructures of mudbrick strengthened with a timber framework (**32**). The building nearest to Tsountas' House had been damaged by the earthquake of the third quarter of the thirteenth century, burying a young man under the debris of the north wall. It had also been affected in part by the fire which destroyed Tsountas' House, without, however, this spreading widely further south. The upper storey of the house was decorated with frescoes of which only fragments survived fallen into a corridor running along its west side and into the space to the north. The former include the nearly life-size painting called the 'Lady of Mycenae' (Mykenaia) and two paintings of figure-of-eight shaped shields.

Higher up the slope in House Gamma, a small room Gamma 3, heavily overbuilt in Hellenistic times, proved to be a kitchen, with ash and cooking vessels on its floor (**54**, exhibited in the site museum). The untouched spots such as the fill in Beta 1, the floor deposits in Gamma 3, other deposits in houses Zeta and Kappa and the odd corner here and there yielded enough pottery and other evidence to give suggestions for dating. The publication of this material is awaited but the preliminary accounts indicate that some buildings were irreparably damaged by the earthquake which left its traces all over Mycenae and by the later conflagration. Yet overall they did not meet an abrupt or violent end but were abandoned and left to fall into ruin and decay.

The houses at the south end of the Quarter, where the fortification wall turns east along the crest of the Chavos ravine, were adapted more or less to the line of the wall. They have a slightly different orientation, less regular ground plans and thinner rubble walls. Their pottery, among which a small krater with pictorial decoration, of quadrupeds, birds and a man, dates their construction to the late thirteenth century, perhaps somewhat later than the rest. They show no traces of burning or demolition other than heavy Hellenistic overbuilding and exposure after the excavation.

The North Quarter (18) is the area most recently (1984-5) re-excavated by Mylonas and Iakovides. To this complex belong the buildings in the area enclosed by the curve of the Cyclopean fortification wall above and to the north-east of the Lion Gate. On the east it is bounded by a strong straight wall running parallel to the row of rooms Lambda and House M in the north part of the citadel.

The site was first excavated in 1890 by Tsountas who cleared it down to bedrock, leaving untouched only a large baulk straddling rooms II 1 and II 2 and a few strips and corners. He gave a very brief account of the excavation proper, mentioning a fill with pot sherds, ash and animal bones, earth floors laid on stone packing into which six children's graves were sunk during the early Geometric period and commenting on the lack of timber framework in the stone walls. The latter were preserved to a height of c.2m with no openings for doors, which led him to believe that the rooms were storage basements accessible only from above. He also lists and illustrates some of his more important finds, such as two hoards of bronze objects (various tools and implements, weapons, a piece of an ingot, and two violin bow fibulae), two terra-cotta bull's heads, a small bronze statuette of the Reshef type known in the Levant and two fragmentary plaques bearing the cartouche of Amenophis III. He dates the whole 'to the transition from the proper Mycenaean period to the next'.

The recent work shows that the area is occupied by three buildings: House N taking up the south-west part of the space available and divided from the other buildings by narrow lanes, House I to its east and House II located north of building N and to the west of I. House I consists of two rooms and an open court in a row, all trapezoidal in shape in order to adapt to the space between Houses N and II on one side and the boundary wall on the other. One more child burial was found in the stone-packed floor of the room I 2, which had also two column or pillar bases along its axis. House II consists of two rectangular rooms side by side. The walls of the east one were strengthened by a timber framework construction. An open court lay between each of the rooms and the fortification wall to the N. There are as well two small rectangular rooms (II 5 and II 6) with their respective court (II 7) attached to the west side of II 2.

The investigation of the areas untouched by Tsountas and the substantial drains produced a quantity of pot sherds of the middle and later years of the thirteenth century and various other typical finds including a number of pan and cover roof tiles. The area was damaged by the earthquake (signs of which are obvious) and abandoned. In Hellenistic times the area was occupied again at a much higher level by buildings with a slightly different orientation; a cistern was built into the fill of court I 3, and there were typical finds such as loom weights, pottery and a coin of Argos of the third century BC.

House M and the adjacent buildings (19) form a triangular sector some 50 yards from the corner of the citadel wall to the east of the North Quarter. Here

Tsountas had cleared to the level of the Hellenistic overbuilding but Mylonas completed the work to reveal a complex of structures including several groups of storerooms lying to the east and north-west of House M. The buildings are separated from the citadel wall to the north by a wide corridor which lies between two high terraces so that the actual passageway is at least 6ft (2m) deep.

House M itself lies on the terrace to the south of the corridor but at an angle to it (and to the citadel wall). The ground floor was divided into four rooms and it had a well-made staircase leading to the upper floor. The entrance to the ground floor is at the north-west corner of the building and is flanked by a double porter's lodge.

Interesting finds from this area include two fragments of an Egyptian plaque like those from the North Quarter and the Room with the Fresco (**colour plate 17**), an inscribed sherd from an open bowl and a small figure with her hands clasped over her breasts.

The storerooms at the east are all interconnected and form a single group of similar chambers. Three of them were constructed side by side within the core of the fortification wall and a fourth, smaller room was built beside the wall and roofed with a corbel vault. Probably all were vaulted in this way and can compare with the well-known and better preserved store rooms at Tiryns. Like the casemates of the lower citadel at Tiryns these 'galleries' remained in use until the final destruction of the citadel.

The Palace (20-22) (**20-23**) complex occupied the summit of the hill, an extensive uneven plateau which slopes relatively gently to the east but has sheer sides to the north, west and south. The plan of phases IV (**14** bottom) & V (**20**) – which we can see today – used the hill in a quite different way from the previous phases (**14** top two plans). Now the buildings stood at different levels and were partly supported on a massive artificial terrace running east to west, roughly following the line of the slope. The area was first tested by Schliemann, then excavated by Tsountas. Wace in the 1920s tested further and had the area planned. Mylonas (with Iakovides and Shear) made further full and detailed studies. Restoration has taken place at various stages, notably when the missing section of the Megaron terrace was restored in 1952-4, but the area is still vulnerable to the weather and work has had to be carried out as recently as 1998-9.

There were two approaches to *The Palace* (20), the earlier on the north and a later official entrance on the south (though there may have been an earlier approach on this side too). From the north the area was reached by two roads. One began at the Lion Gate and from the south end of the Great Ramp wound its way up the west slope; the other started at the North Gate and ran west along the north wall of the citadel. They meet *c*.90 yards west of the North Gate where a staircase was constructed in a fissure in the rock. The two roadways can be traced at intervals. In a second stage of development the area at the base of the steps was converted into a paved courtyard. At the top there was a landing and the stair is presumed to have continued. It can next be traced at the stepped beginning of a ramp supported by a series of curved retaining walls which end at the North-west Propylon.

Four small rectangular rooms lay on the north at a lower level. The two at the west lie between the terrace wall and the rock slope; they interconnect and appear

43/44 Ivory group of two women and a boy from the north side of the palace area (39-165,166,167 NM 7711; height 3in, 7.8cm). © Mycenae Archive: Emil Seraf

45 *Plaster head of a man from the north side of the palace area (39-164 NM 7712; height 2.5in, 6.5cm).* © Mycenae Archive: Charles K. Williams II

to have been entered from the west. For this reason they have been thought to have formed some kind of guardroom – but possibly, on analogy with the palace of Nestor at Pylos, they might have formed an archive room. Those at the east are at an oblique angle and underlie the later temple terrace; here the deep foundations rest on the rock. Both pairs are noted for the finds associated with them: a floor deposit of pottery on the floor of the western with loomweights and handleless cups containing pigments *under* it; a deposit of possible cult significance *over* the eastern (including the ivory group (**43 & 44**) and the stucco head (**45**) on display in the National Museum in Athens).

The actual entrance is formed by a propylon. There was a central door and a column on a conglomerate base (at the south a double one) on the central axis in either porch. To the north the propylon overlooked a small cobbled terrace, with a wider open space beyond. A further small court lay to the south and from this a stepped entrance led into the north corridor.

The area between the north corridor and the north terrace wall, the highest terrace of the palace complex, is almost completely denuded, partly from its position and partly because it served as the foundation for the later temples. Traces of structures dating to several building phases exist but are difficult to restore even on paper.

The entrance passage at the west continued south past the end of the middle terrace of the complex to the entry known as the Western Portal, another structure of propylon type with a handsome conglomerate threshold. Immediately inside this entry on the north side another conglomerate threshold led into a square room, again of indeterminable function. Further east lay an area now plausibly suggested to have been an open terrace court in front of the higher rooms to the north.

The South corridor was in the last phase of the palace blocked at the east end and led nowhere. Earlier it sloped up to a large threshold over which access would have been possible to the east end of the middle terrace, now almost completely denuded.

A second passage led with a dog leg from within the Western Portal to the Great Court. Immediately north of this, leading from the Court upwards to the west, was a flight of stairs; the space beneath opened to the west as a storage area. These stairs indicate that at least this part of the palace was of two storeys or that access to the roof terrace was required. The floor of the Court was decorated with multi-coloured stucco. The north wall was faced with ashlar cut poros stone held to the rubble backing by wooden tie beams; there was a painted dado representing decorative stone work of triglyphs and half rosettes (**23**). To the south, there was probably only a low parapet allowing a general view of the Argive plain; to the east lay the main Megaron of the Palace of which the south-west corner tumbled down into the ravine below but has been restored.

The Megaron complex consists of a columned porch, a vestibule and the main room. The porch was shallow, opening onto the courtyard: it had two columns at the front, a floor made of gypsum slabs, and a small passage on the north leading to steps by which a room decorated with wall-paintings depicting draperies and equipped with benches, a hearth and a staircase beyond could be reached. This is considered to have been the approach in the final building phase to the domestic quarters of the Palace at the east end of the middle terrace. At the south end of the porch was a decorated base and a basin for libations. A large single-leafed door led to the vestibule; only the threshold has survived, made of a single block of conglomerate with two small square holes at the ends which were meant to accommodate the wooden posts of the jambs. The vestibule had a floor of painted stucco bordered with gypsum slabs, and a doorway leading to the Megaron. To the right of the door is a raised slab similar to those in the palace of Nestor at Pylos. The Megaron itself, almost square in shape, was the principal room in the palace. The floor was decorated with coloured stucco and bordered with gypsum slabs on all four sides and the walls were covered with frescoes notably a battle scene and one of women in front of a building. In the middle of the room, there was a large round hearth; its painted stucco surface was renewed ten times, but the decorative motifs of flames and spirals remained unchanged. The hearth was encircled by four wooden columns, probably clad in bronze, which supported the roof; their stone bases have survived. On analogy with the other palaces, the throne probably stood against the middle of the south wall. For vivid reconstructions of the appearance of the Megaron complex see Mylonas 1983.

Opposite the Megaron, on the west side of the Court, there is a square room with double doors leading to an irregular forecourt. From this forecourt at least one door opened directly onto the Court. This complex, once thought to be the throne room, has been identified as the Guest Suite with a bathroom to the west.

The Grand Staircase was the official access to the palace, this time from the south-west and was the last feature to be built. It was a four-sided structure which contained a spacious, imposing staircase divided into two flights, a stone one which has survived with a wooden one above. The wooden flight rose parallel to the stone flight and reached a landing that crossed over the top of the staircase to lead into the forecourt of the Guest Suite.

The Artisans' Quarter (21) lies on the east slope of the upper citadel. Here the rock slopes down in a series of three terraces. All are thought to have been part of the total palace complex, thus making that at Mycenae by far the largest of the three of which we have the plans. The uppermost terrace, immediately beyond the presumed domestic quarters of the palace, is almost completely denuded; on the second and third, however, were preserved basements of the Mycenaean period below extensive Hellenistic overbuilding.

What has come to be called the Artisans' Quarter is an extensive building complex, almost square in shape, which originally had two and perhaps more storeys. It is bounded on the east by a strong retaining wall separating it from the House of Columns. The thickness and timber framing of the walls, the fallen debris which included fresco fragments, and a staircase in the north-west corner give evidence of the upper storey.

In its present form the building consists of two sections separated by a narrow open court from which rain water was drained off through the citadel wall. At the north end of this was the stair and the entry to the building itself by a small ramp. To the west of the court there was a narrow covered corridor roughly the same length as the court itself. To the south of this corridor lay an irregular room which at this level opened only onto an external passage by the citadel wall. A row of four rooms lay beyond the corridor and this room to the west; all appear to have been basements entered from above. To the east of the court lay another corridor and beyond it four more rooms which do not communicate with one another nor with the internal corridor though they do seem to have opened onto the side passage of the House of Columns though at a much higher level (**24**). At the north end of the east corridor was a short passage at right angles which communicated directly with the House of Columns (though it was later sealed off). Intact floor deposits lay under the burnt debris on the floors. This included, as well as whole pots, ivory chips (debitage) and off-cuts, fragments of gold sheet, slag from bronze smelting and fragments of semi-precious stones. From these finds the building is identified as the workshop of the palace craftsmen and the plan clearly resembles that of a medieval souk.

The House of Columns (22) lies on the lowest terrace of the east slope between the Artisans' Quarter and the east Cyclopean wall. It has a central court surrounded by a colonnade (hence the name). It too is thought to have belonged to the palace complex. In the earliest phase there was direct communication with the workshops to the west. The only remains are basements and the foundations of the ground floor. One can still see quite clearly the entrance marked by the bases of the door jambs, made of conglomerate (one of these still shows traces of the saw with which it was cut) and the wide threshold of the outer door. Crossing this threshold one enters a narrow passage which ends in the central court, on the north side of which there is a large square megaron-like room, which in the reoccupation period after the burnt destruction was divided into smaller rooms. The megaron had a central hearth and a piece of a chimney was found nearby. A passage from the far right-hand corner leads to other rooms (or possibly a single larger room). The eastern section of the house is in a poor state of preservation but there is evidence of another large room, possibly of megaron type. At the south side of the court, the basement storerooms still survive with other rooms above them entered from the court. From the basement level came one of the few inscribed Linear B tablets from within the citadel listing cloths of an unknown type (**61**). Other finds include pithoi and transport stirrup jars.

The building lay on a massive artificial terrace which covered earlier buildings. The pottery from the fill gives a construction date in the second half of the thirteenth century BC. The house was destroyed by fire after which the entry to the Artisans' Quarter was sealed off and smaller structures built over the main rooms.

The House of Columns was the principal building of this wing of the palace complex, but it has not been possible to determine with any certainty exactly what purpose it served.

House Delta (23) marks the east end of a triangular yard to the north of the Artisans' Quarter and the House of Columns. It was an irregular four-sided structure which occupied the whole area between this clearing and the citadel wall. It faces the yard with a low open veranda; an inlet in the north-west corner marks a drain that runs under the passage between it and the House of Columns before exiting through the citadel wall. The rooms behind the veranda are built in relation to the citadel wall as it was before the construction of the North-east Extension. They are basements which as often communicate neither with each other nor with the outside. There are two rows of three rooms and a further row of two rooms at the south; in the western of these are the remains of a staircase, but there is no evidence for the plan of the upper floor. Dating evidence (from sherds) is similar to that of the other adjacent structures.

House Gamma (24) lies on the north side of the triangular yard and was built along the road that runs parallel to the north citadel wall at an oblique angle to House Delta to the south. The rooms preserved are at basement level and were adapted to the configuration of the rock which is very uneven at this point. At the east end there is a rock outcrop rising sharply which restricted the building but which seems, with the basement terrace, to have served to support the upper storey. The plan is unusual and not easy to understand. The entire width of the west end is occupied by an L-shaped room, the long narrow section of which resembles a corridor while the other section is almost square. To the east there is a row of three small rooms, followed by four more which, though wider, are somewhat irregular because of the rock outcrop. The penultimate one is very narrow indeed. The angle of the L-shaped room on the south-west is occupied by two more rooms at right angles to the rest. The walls are preserved to a good height and in places floor deposits were still intact. The occupation history is similar to that of the other adjacent structures.

The North Storerooms (25) (**61**) lie beside the roadway running from the North Gate along a terrace, supported on the north by a retaining wall, to the triangular yard to the east. They faced the roadway and backed against the rock slope at the south. The row, of at least four storerooms, contained jars in situ which, as one had been mended in antiquity with a little clay, would seem to have been used for dry products such as cereals. Some pithoi have been replaced in situ and can be seen. Other vases were found on the floors as well as items in considerable quantity from the upper storey (including two fragments of an inscribed Linear B tablet recording barley, flour and cyperus), all sealed by burnt destruction debris. This forms one of the best groups of evidence for the history of the citadel. The building was overlaid by a fill of LH IIIC date and used as a terrace for another roadway connecting the North Gate and the North-east Extension by way of the triangular clearing.

The North (or Postern) Gate (26) as it stands today was constructed late in the second phase of the fortification of the citadel, but it seems likely that there had been some earlier means of exit at the north–east corner (**16**) to give direct access to the water supply, to the routes leading north and north–east from the acropolis and to serve a growing community outside the walls to the north. The gate was restored with the citadel wall by the Anastylosis Service. Beyond the gate to the west there is a small open court from which a path, narrowing gradually, led to the northern approach to the palace.

This second gate was a faithful replica of the Lion Gate, built in an opening deliberately made into the north wall for this purpose. On the one side, a bastion of conglomerate blocks was constructed parallel to the opposite section of the old wall. A narrow passage was thus formed between them, similar to the outer courtyard of the Lion Gate, and the gate erected at the end of it. Here again the frame consisted of four conglomerate blocks forming a doorway 6ft (2m) high, 6' wide and 4' (1.5m) deep. On either side of the threshold and lintel one can still see the pivot holes for the hinges of the two leaves of the wooden doors (now represented by a modern replica), as well as the two holes in the jambs for the great wooden bolt beam that kept the door shut. A drain runs out beneath the threshold. The only difference between the North Gate and the Lion Gate is that instead of the single relief slab in the relieving triangle above the lintel, there are two conglomerate slabs with an empty space between them (which helps to relieve the weight considerably) and with a slightly convex lower surface, so that only the two ends actually rest on the lintel, where it is supported by the jambs.

On the inner side of the gate, there is a small niche as at the Lion Gate. The stairway which led from the main path to the west to another linking to the North Storerooms and the east end of the acropolis runs over this niche.

Underground Cistern (27): fresh water springs existed in the hills east of the citadel; there was no difficulty in channelling the water through conduits to the foot of the hill, but there was no way of raising the water to the higher sections of the citadel nor of cutting the hard rock in order to provide a suitable cistern within the original fortified area. The only suitable place was a crevice in the rock at the north-east corner of the old wall. Study of the building history of the North-east Extension now suggests that the cistern was originally outside the walls (**16**) when it would have been approached by a path from the exit on the north of the citadel. The date of its construction cannot be suggested but there is no reason to suppose that it was not an early feature. Late in the thirteenth century however, either from fashion or from necessity, systems to ensure the safety of the water supply were constructed not only at Mycenae but at Tiryns and at Athens as well. At Mycenae this meant extending the fortification walls to enclose the natural terrace at the far east end of the citadel and constructing an entrance passage to the cistern through the wall. The new descent runs under the wall, covered by a corbel vault and leads down to a Cyclopean portal in the outer face of the fortification wall. The lintel of this became cracked on the west and was supported by a monolithic pillar. This portal opened onto a landing. From here, probably the original entry, there followed a further stretch of the descent, corbel vaulted throughout and divided into two sections. The second section has its walls coated with hydraulic cement and ends up in the underground cistern itself, which was supplied with water from the Perseia spring by a system of pipes. At both Tiryns and Athens the water systems remained in use for only a relatively short period of time and then each was used as a refuse dump during LH IIIC Middle (i.e. the late twelfth century BC). There is no surviving evidence for the later history of the Mycenae cistern.

The North Sally Port (28) runs obliquely through the wall and is low and narrow. It was once believed to have been a drain but can be shown to have been an exit by the method of construction and the wear on the inner and outer thresholds.

The South Sally Port (29) is the larger and runs directly through the wall at right angles. It has usually been thought to be a secret emergency exit. It is, however, quite visible even from a great distance and seems to have led to an outer terrace overlooking the ravine. Iakovides suggests that this terrace 'served the ends of both security and relaxation'.

These two openings acted as protection to the North Gate and the water supply but would have been easily blocked in case of a emergency.

House Alpha (30) is one of two structures within the area of the North-east Extension and lies at the south side of the enclosed space. Only the basements survive and it was badly damaged by a trench excavated by Schliemann. It appears to be built directly against the citadel wall. Six storage jars were found in situ in the south rather irregular room which was entered from the east beside the fortification wall. A terra-cotta bathtub lay in the other to the west. The house probably extended further but nothing has been found. No dating evidence has been published.

House Beta (31) is a large structure to the north of House Alpha, rectangular in plan with an extension to the east apparently abutting against the citadel wall. There are four rooms: a large rectangular room to the north, two narrow rooms along the south side and the blind extension to the east. The entrance was at the south-west corner and opened onto the first of the narrow rooms. Pottery in situ in the room by the fortification wall should be assigned to the earthquake horizon in the third quarter of the thirteenth century. This evidence and the fact that the west end of the house seems to have been altered when the approach to the cistern was laid out suggest that the house was in use and damaged well before the North-east Extension was built. There is no actual evidence to support Mylonas' very plausible suggestion that control of the water supply was carried out from this house and the hypothesis does not depend on the house being within the walls throughout its period of use. In the Hellenistic period it was used again as a foundation.

8 The material world

Preservation

Only certain materials survive from antiquity, so any description of artifacts produced by the Mycenaeans cannot avoid being unbalanced. Pottery, for instance, survives well but sherds were often ignored by early excavators, notably by Tsountas in his extensive excavations at Mycenae; metal was regularly recycled in ancient times and is subject to very different rates of corrosion and decay; wood and cereal grains are preserved only when charred; textiles do not survive in the climate of Greece. In addition to these complications it is clear that some products were produced only for the elite in a system that seems to have been centrally controlled. Others were common and generally available. Some were for use in daily life of whatever social stratum, others were confined to funerary use.

Another factor which has affected our knowledge is the extremely uneven pattern of discovery. We have already seen that almost no tholos tombs escaped looting. Though at Mycenae we have a very large number of chamber tombs, at Tiryns very few have been discovered. Just as uneven is the evidence from the palaces: at both Mycenae and Tiryns almost nothing has survived of their furnishings, stores or records; Pylos, though much better preserved, is quite clearly provincial in character and with the presence of texts skews the evidence in a very peculiar way. At Thebes, on the other hand, we may debate the plan and the chronology but we have a very considerable quantity of artifacts as well as texts. Thus the evidence is very mixed, partly three-dimensional and partly derived from texts.

Where to see the finds

The objects which have been found at Mycenae are now divided unequally between the National Museum in Athens and the site museum at Mycenae (the latter formerly in the provincial capital, Nauplion). A few notable items are in international collections, for instance one column from the façade of the Treasury of Atreus collected by Lord Sligo is now in the British Museum. In Athens are the finds from Schliemann's excavations of Grave Circle A and on the acropolis, the richer items from Grave Circle B, all finds from the chamber tombs excavated by Tsountas and from his work on the acropolis, a selection of material from the excavations of the British School (chamber tombs 1920s, Ivory Houses etc. 1950s) and most wall paintings from all periods of work. This spectacular display must always be viewed together with the less striking objects which remained in the Argolid in assessing the

range of art and production as a whole. The unique feature of the collection in the site museum is the material from the Cult Centre, a fascinating mixture of material both elite and mundane.

Elite items

One of the important factors in identifying Mycenae through archaeology as a 'capital' is the quantity of high status, high quality products found and the fact that, by the thirteenth century at least, some are unique to Mycenae. Goods of this type occur frequently in the tombs of the Early Palatial period in many if not most areas of Greece but, by the Palatial period, tombs in general appear to be less rich. This is not, however, a reflection of the contemporary economy but of burial practice. Consumption of elite products seems to have been regulated probably by the palace bureaucracy and normally only a carefully restricted set of basics formed part of burial assemblages (for the pottery repertoire see **28**). Our evidence for high quality products at this time thus comes from non-funerary contexts with the House of Shields at Mycenae as one of the most prolific.

46   Ivory head of a man wearing a boar's tusk helmet from the House of Shields, thirteenth century BC (53-405 NM 7397; height 2.8in, 7.2cm). © Mycenae Archive: E.B. French

Three types of high quality goods were identified there (**27**, **46-8**, **colour plate 11**): furnishings inlaid with ivory and coloured stone, stone vases and faience vases. Furnishings of this kind, which include small boxes as well as larger items, have been found elsewhere (notably at Thebes) but the stone vases and elaborate faience vessels are known almost exclusively from Mycenae. It has been suggested that the faience in particular is produced by itinerant craftsmen working in mixed techniques (Peltenberg in Gale 1991). It is also suggested that the craftsmen themselves might have been loaned as a 'royal gift' from one monarch to another and that these materials illustrate well the distinction between gift economy and commodity economy both of which were current in the Palatial period.

Other elite symbols notable at Mycenae are the major examples of sculpture. The stelai of the shaft graves (**7**) are primitive in composition and execution; the latter partly due to the poor medium of shelly sandstone which carves irregularly. But by the Palatial period mastery in carving has been achieved. The Lion Gate relief is unique (**front cover**). The facade of the Treasury of Atreus (**26**) with its elaborate columns and decorated relieving triangle is of a type and quality paralleled only by

47 *Ivory plaque showing a lion eating a calf from the House of Shields, thirteenth century
BC (53-408 NM 7400; width 2in, 5.2cm).* © Mycenae Archive: E.B. French

48 *Stone vessels of steatite from the House of Shields, thirteenth century BC (53-115
NM 7389, height 5.85in, 15cm; 53-788 NM 7591, height 7.8in, 20cm; 53-114
(with 113 lid) MM 29096, height 7in, 18cm).* © Mycenae Archive: E.B. French

*49 Ivory plaque of two confronted sphinxes (standing on a possible shrine with central
column and horns of consecration) from the House of Sphinxes, thirteenth century BC
(53-211 NM 7525; height 3.15in, 8cm).* © Mycenae Archive: E.B. French

the ceiling of the side chamber of the tholos at Orchomenos. (The decoration of the
Tomb of Clytemnestra was possibly more simple and gypsum which is less hard
wearing was chosen as the medium, making a quality assessment difficult.) Other
stone carving of this quality has been found in the Palace (such fragments as have
been found are exhibited in the site museum) and there are scattered pieces from later
debris levels throughout the site. At a smaller scale use was made of a tubular drill
(**17**) with water or an abrasive (like emery from Naxos) and the fine sharpness of tiny
obsidian blades was used particularly for ivory.

The various ivories both free-standing and decorative show a similar mastery in
carving. (This was doubtless also true of wood but though there are many small
fragments no single item is preserved.) There are from Mycenae three outstanding
pieces of ivory carved in the round: one, the so-called ivory trio of two women and
a boy (?) (**43 & 44**) from just north of the palace area is now displayed in Athens;
two from the Cult Centre are in the site museum, a couchant lion and a small ivory

*50 Canaanite amphora with a 'butterfly'
mark on the shoulder in matt red
paint from the storeroom of the South
House Annex, late thirteenth century
BC (54-601 MM 16750; height
19.5in, 50cm).*
© Mycenae Archive: E.B. French

head (**colour plates 13 & 14**). This last was almost certainly the head of a cult statue displayed on the altar in front of the fresco in the Room with the Fresco. Various standards of workmanship are found in the smaller pieces but some of the decorative panels for boxes like the sphinx plaque (**49**) from which the House of Sphinxes is named and the lion and calf from the House of Shields (**47**) show what could be achieved. (Almost all this material is displayed in Athens.) Also of ivory there were handles for mirrors (with bronze disks), combs and pins. All of these are most often found in early tombs but several combs and pins have come from the Citadel House Area (e.g. **40** 68-1510). How practical the combs were is another matter.

Carving of great competence was also required to make the moulds for gold and glass jewellery of which seven (Burns p.171) (two in the site museum (**colour plate 19**), four in Athens, one in Boston) of the 25 known from the Aegean are from Mycenae. The use of such moulds extends in time and purpose from the shaft graves (the discs, **9**) to the Cult Centre (the beehive beads, **colour plate 18**). But surprisingly the Mycenaeans of the Palatial period did not use their skills to make seal stones in hard stone though they continued to use such seals regularly for marking and sealing items in their store-rooms (**60**). The actual seals cut at this period are of soft stone and of distinctly inferior quality. Moreover on present evidence these were not used administratively.

Actual imports too can be taken as elite symbols – possibly of the merchandising known as gift exchange – but almost the only type of imported item in the thirteenth century is the Canaanite amphora (**50**, on display in the site museum) from the Levant. The one tested by residue analysis contained resinated wine! A few pieces of

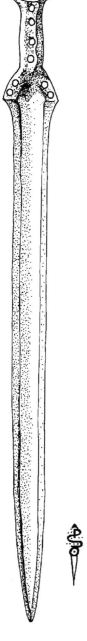

51 *Bronze sword of the Naue II type from the House of the Warrior Vase found by Schliemann (NM 1017; length 25.6in, 65cm)*

white shaved ware from Cyprus have been found at Mycenae and a wider though still small range of pottery imports have been identified at Tiryns. A recent survey (Cline 1994) lists some 50 'orientalia' (i.e. from Egypt, the Levant, Mesopotamia or Anatolia) from Mycenae itself in contexts of the Palatial period as a whole out of a total of 900 for the period 1600-1100 BC in the Aegean (including of course Crete). But this list is misleading: it covers both the prolific Early Palatial as well as both halves of the Palatial period proper; it includes items which *may* be locally made by foreign craftsmen as well as those which are totally out of context – for instance a surprising small group of Egyptian Early Dynastic pieces which probably came to the mainland via Crete. There are, in fact, no remotely complete imports from overseas in the thirteenth century though there are a couple of oddities, as well as some scarabs (**colour plate 8**) and some fragments of alabaster vases (including three from the House of Shields), though these may have been kept after breakage as stock material. It would seem that the palatial control that restricted display in thirteenth-century chamber tombs may have also affected the import of elite items. Perhaps, however, there was some other disturbance to trade in both worked and raw materials (timber and metals) which would always have made up the bulk of the trade. The most intriguing items of all are the faience plaques (**colour plate 17**) of Anemhotep III found in several later contexts right across the site, including the Cult Centre. These may be treaty documentation or calling cards of the ambassador whose trip may be noted in the famous 'Aegean List' – an inscription on a statue base from the funerary temple of Amenhotep III at Kom el-Hatan that lists places in the Aegean world.

The same retrieval situation applies to weapons and armour (which must be considered overall elite items): we have more actual evidence from deposition in early tombs than we have from the thirteenth century itself. A typical panoply for a Mycenaean consisted of a couple of swords, sometimes elaborately decorated, a dagger and a spear. The inherent weakness of both swords and daggers where the blade joins the hilt led to various improvements over time, but about the middle of the thirteenth century a new type of sword first appears which seems to be an innovation from Central Europe: a longer stronger weapon with a flanged hilt known as the Naue II sword. Schliemann found an example in the upper levels of the House of the Warrior Vase (**51**) and hilt plates for this type came from the ivory deposit in Room 32 of the Cult Centre (exhibited in the site museum). The way such swords would have been used seems to indicate a change in battle practice: slashing instead of thrusting. Body armour is very rare though an almost complete set was found in a tomb at Dendra (exhibited in the Nauplion Museum). This consisted of a basic cuirass to which were added shoulder pieces, arm guards, and skirt sections to protect the lower body front and back. All seem to have been lined in cloth or leather to prevent chafing. There was also a separate high collar to shield the face. The set included two greaves and a hand guard for the right hand or sword hand (another similar piece came from Chamber Tomb 15 at Mycenae). Other similar finds have been rare – a shoulder piece found in another tomb at Dendra in the 1930s was mistaken for a helmet! Though it is possible to fight and manoeuvre in this armour (we had a full replica of the same weight, 55lb or 25kg, made to test this) it would have been cumbersome as well as expensive; many may instead have used layered leather. The helmet was indeed of leather though often covered with boar's tusk plates arranged decoratively in a manner later described by Homer (**46**). This type of helmet was in use right through the Mycenaean period from the sixteenth to the twelfth century but there is some slight evidence that a cuirass (of Near Eastern type) with many small bronze plates sewn onto a leather or cloth backing came into use in the twelfth century.

For shields unfortunately the only evidence comes from illustration on wall paintings, seals and pictorial pottery and from small models in ivory. On the Lion Hunt dagger from shaft grave IV (**colour plate 7**) two different types of shield are shown: the 'tower' shield, a large rectangular type which seems to be the earlier as it is the only type shown in the wall paintings on Thera, and the 'figure-of-eight' type. Both types were probably made from leather over a wicker frame as they are shown dappled to represent the patterning of the hide. In the twelfth century a smaller round shield was introduced carried by the warriors on the Warrior Vase (**colour plate 20**).

Products in general use

The most ubiquitous find is pottery (**13, 28, 54**). It survives well and though restorable vases are much more commonly found in tombs, one horizon of the settlement both inside and outside the citadel, probably the result of an earthquake in the second half of the thirteenth century, has left on the floors of buildings a large number of complete or restorable pots. The use of the wheel for the manufacture of pottery was widespread, but not universal, from the beginning of the Middle Helladic period. By the Palatial period only a few specialised vessels were handmade, possibly for reasons of their usage. The clay is well prepared except when deliberately tempered for larger vessels or for those intended for cooking which needed to resist heat (**54**). Many of the shapes are elaborate and required skilled manufacture, particularly two of the most ubiquitous, the kylix and the stirrup jar. The surfaces in the Early Palatial

52 *Transport Stirrup Jar inscibed in the Linear B script from near the Poros Wall to the east of the Tomb of Clytemnestra, thirteenth century BC: MY Z 202 reading Je-ra, ka-ta-ro (52-499 NM 7628; height 16in, 41cm).* © Mycenae Archive: E.B. French

53 *Pestle and mortar (in a hard compact stone suitable for grinding seeds and condiments) from the House of Sphinxes, thirteenth century BC (55-255,256 MM 8482,3; heights 3.15in, 8cm; 5in, 13cm).* © Mycenae Archive: E.B. French

period are still often burnished but by Palatial times a speedier technique, probably dipping the completed vessel in a lime wash to give differential firing temperature to the surface layer, was used. The decoration, by the thirteenth century, is almost entirely dark (red to dark brown) on a light background. The paint is in fact a fine coloured clay. Throughout, the studs or other features of metal vessels are occasionally imitated in the pottery counterparts. Mycenaean pottery can be divided into three main classes on the basis of the fabric and the decoration: painted fine ware (**13, 28**), unpainted fine ware and cooking ware (**54**). In addition there are larger vessels where temper (grit) has been added to give extra strength to the pot. Two classes of these – transport stirrup jars (**52**) and huge storage pithoi (**54**) – are decorated, the former with paint either in a dark on light or light on dark technique and the latter with impressed or incised applied motifs which as well as being decorative are useful in giving a good grip when the pot has to be moved. Unpainted wares (**54**) are of various qualities; there are some superbly finished kylikes from all phases but other pieces are more utilitarian and some quite clearly mass-produced at a 'throw-away' standard. The clay for cooking wares was specially chosen and was tempered with scraps of volcanic rock (probably wastage from mortars of stone, cf **53**, though this is of a finer hard stone, from Methana or Thera) to help the vessels withstand the high temperatures of cooking. The shapes of cooking ware are simple but practical (**54**): one and two handled jars with a narrowed neck, dippers, tripod vessels of at least three different body shapes sometimes with lids, griddles, 'souvlaki' trays, lamps or braziers. There is one specialised oven or stand (exhibited in the site museum). Painted pottery, though always a small proportion of the total sherdage in any excavation unit, is often very beautifully and elaborately decorated in the Early Palatial period (**13b**). Later the decoration becomes much more stylised and almost all traces of the Cretan origins of the motifs disappear. The treatment becomes very schematic and antithetic designs predominate (**28**).

Because it is so prolific we can chart the changes in shape and decoration of Mycenaean pottery very closely. Thus we are able to use pottery evidence to suggest the date of destruction of the buildings in which it is found. This aspect of pottery studies has in the past obscured the more basic importance of pottery as a functional utensil. Recent work however has begun to redress this. Groups of pots, a jug and krater with kylikes for instance, have been identified as drinking sets and some of these groups are interrelated by their decoration (**13e**). A problem that remains intriguing and has not been solved is the introduction and sudden popularity of certain shapes; that known as the deep bowl (**28** top right, bottom left) – a deep porridge bowl often with the base very heavily worn by an action like stirring – is quite unrelated to anything previously known but becomes overwhelmingly popular at the beginning of the thirteenth century and remains a 'type artifact' until the final destruction of Mycenae. The scientific technique of residue analysis (of which more below p.132) suggests that at Thebes this shape was used sometimes for drink and sometimes for food. Other pots were clearly intended for storage/transport. The heavy stirrup jars (**52**) are now generally referred to as transport stirrup jars and probably carried oil or wine. The small fine stirrup jars (**28c**) have always been supposed to be the containers

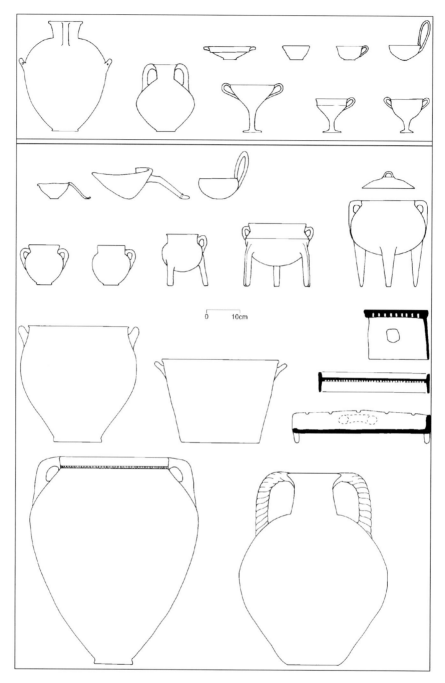

54 *Unpainted and domestic pottery.* © Mycenae Archive.
Top from left to right: **unpainted ware**: *hydria, shallow angular bowl, handleless cup, cup, dipper, amphora, conical kylix, carinated kylix, rounded kylix.*
Below: **cooking ware**: *dipper/lamp, lamp/brazier, dipper, cooking pot jar and jug, tripod vessels (one with lid), krater, vat, oven, griddle, Souvlaki dish.*
Bottom: **heavy/coarse ware**: *pithos, storage amphora*

for the heavily exported perfumed oil, the manufacture of which is documented on the Linear B tablets from Pylos. This assumption has recently been brought into question by the residue analysis of the contents of one such stirrup jar from the Cult Centre at Mycenae which had contained wine (sealed by a layer of olive oil). Some transport Stirrup Jars bear inscriptions in the Linear B script; others are marked with a single character (which does not count as an inscription; these are not included on the plan, **61**). Very occasionally fine or heavy pots bear inscriptions or symbols; two are exhibited in the site museum: a deep bowl from near House M and a large jar from the Room with the Fresco which originally contained wine.

One particular type of pottery seems to have been produced very largely for export: pictorial pottery (**55**). The type is extremely popular in Cyprus where the large decorated kraters, probably used as the centre pieces in drinking ceremonies, are widely found in tombs of those whom we may suppose to have been a nouveau riche bourgeoisie. Such vessels are known throughout the Palatial period. Some seem to have depicted real scenes or myths, others to be symbolic. Chariot kraters are some of the most conspicuous and pastoral scenes with bulls are very popular on Cyprus though not at Mycenae. It has been suggested that the site of Berbati (in the valley to the east of Mycenae) which has excellent clay sources was a specialist centre of manufacture for this export trade but the scientific evidence does not yet allow this to be definitely confirmed. In the Post-Palatial period, particularly after the middle of the twelfth century BC, another pictorial style becomes very prevalent with representations of animals, birds and fish (**66 & 67**).

Clay is also used for other very common artifacts: small terracotta figurines (**29 & 30**), the counterparts of the larger figures (**37**) found in shrines. The small figurines are overwhelmingly female of three types which change through time and not from usage and bovid (identifiable from their horns but almost always sexless). Also found but less common are group figurines of chariots (on exhibit in the site museum), chairs or thrones often with a seated figure, oxen with a figure on the haunches holding reins (which may represent ploughing though this is disputed) and animals of other species. Very rare are horses with riders and toreadors (figures which may be bull leapers holding the horns of oxen) though several of these two types as well as chariots have recently been found at a shrine on the Methana peninsula. Figurines are found in tombs and in shrines but many come from the debris of domestic contexts. It is often suggested that these come from 'house shrines' but there is no evidence for such shrines except the figurines themselves. What is now certain is that figurines were not merely children's toys as was once thought.

The other common artifact of this period is the small stone cone or conulus (**42**), once always called a spindle whorl. The basic type is conical with a central vertical hole but others have a shaped shank and curved base. The stone used is steatite, both a handsome dark grey or red colour or a soft pale green. A recent detailed study of all the conuli from the Citadel House excavations (343 in all of which 178 were from the cult rooms) examined the wear patterns in the hope of identifying the function more clearly. In spite of this study conuli still remain an enigma: some certainly were spindle whorls, others dress or curtain weights but

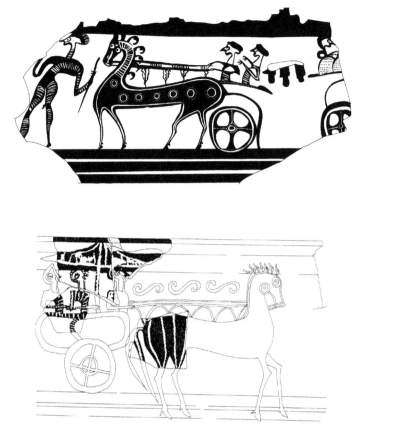

55 *Pictorial pottery of the thirteenth and twelfth centuries BC showing chariots, a boxer,*
fish and goats eating a (symbolic) tree. © Mycenae Archive: Charles K.
Williams II, Anneke Poelstra-Traga, W.D. Taylour, Diana Wardle

there still seem to be too many without some other specific but as yet unidentified function, even granting that they are almost indestructible. Heavy implements of stone were also common: saddle querns, pounders of various shapes and mortars with pestles to go with them (**53**). The mortars were often of volcanic rock though this example is of a fine hard stone for specialised grinding. A surprising quantity of such tools came from the Cult Centre and this class of material deserves more study than it usually receives.

The technology of metalworking was not new and indeed did not change greatly until long after the Middle Ages. The basic processes were hammering and the use of simple moulds. More elaborate items show knowledge of advanced techniques. The dagger blades (**colour plate 7**) and cups were decorated in metals of several colours on a black background long thought to be an enamel-like substance called niello. The most recent scientific work on the collection of items decorated in this way in the National Museum in Athens has shown that the black is not niello but an alloy of bronze with gold and silver. The origin of the technique is not known. Another unknown is what adhesive was used to attach the beading of gold granulation and to attach gold ornaments to textiles or other materials (such as glass). Here the thin gold sheet often bears a blackish deposit on the inside but it has never been possible to have an analysis carried out. Perhaps the most startling of the techniques already known to craftsmen by the seventeenth century BC is enamelling itself. **Colour plate 7** shows a sword hilt from shaft grave IV of Grave Circle A with this decoration.

Though vessels in precious metals or of decorated bronze were found in chamber tombs of the Early Palatial period as well as in the shaft graves, gold and silver cease to be widely found in the Palatial period. A silver cup with inlaid warrior heads (exhibited in Athens) from Tomb 24 in the Kato Phournos cemetery is probably from the first half of this period. It may be supposed that the tholos tombs of which the last three are from the Palatial period would have contained richer goods. The only unrobbed tholos from the Argolid, that at Kokla, dates from the beginning of the period and though mysteriously without a burial contained a handsome set of silver vases.

The practice of tinning pottery to be used in burial rituals which begins in LH II, but continues into the Palatial period, is thought to be a means of giving the appearance of metal vessels in silver without the waste of resources that actually using the metals would have occasioned. There has been discussion as to whether a gold or silver effect was wanted but the find of a tinned vessel with added gold sheet seems to indicate that silver was intended. Mountjoy (1993, 127-8) suggests that these vessels were used in particular for the burial rites when display would have been paramount. The painting of ornaments of terracotta in blue to resemble lapis lazuli, glass or faience, though to my knowledge only noted once by archaeologists (Tomb of the Genii, *BSA* 25,385), would have had a similar purpose.

From fourteenth-century tombs there are, however, several groups of more utilitarian bronze vessels including an important group found by Tsountas in Chamber Tomb 47 (exhibited in Athens; nice examples of this date from the tomb with the armour at Dendra are on exhibit in Nauplion though most others are in Athens).

We must presume that the types continued in use even when they were not deposited in tombs. The shapes we know are: piriform jugs, conical kraters (the kalathos or cauldron), shallow cups, lamps and a shallow tripod vessel (similar to a shape found in cooking ware). Lead too was common and had several uses: large vessels (found widely in 'houses'), weights and clamps for repairing cracked pottery.

The presence of bronze vessels in Grave Circle A has been taken as evidence that they were themselves high status items. However, on ethnographic parallels from village usage in Greece and Turkey in the last 50 years, metal vessels are widely found. They constitute a significant outlay but are extremely long-lasting; moreover they can be recycled or traded in when worn out for repair or replacement – taken in for update if required. It is the deposition of such items, as with tool assemblages and weapons, in tombs that is the mark of status.

What we know of bronze tools comes almost exclusively from two sources: occasional finds in graves and from hoards – groups of material either gathered together in an emergency and buried for later retrieval that never occurred, or the collected property of some bronzesmith which again went astray. Other tools of bone and antler were less likely to be recycled and are found occasionally in primary but mainly in secondary contexts like rubbish dumps. Identification of the usage of tools is often subjective, depending on the resemblance to tools known today in ethnographic contexts. From the chamber tombs at Mycenae (though many of the examples found are certainly of earlier date, the types probably did not vary greatly through time) there are several knives with bone handles, sickles, axes, adzes, cleavers, tweezers, chisels and nails (**colour plate 9**). From a hoard found close to the surround wall at the east of the Tomb of Clytemnestra and probably of thirteenth-century date, as well as lumps of bronze from crucibles, came similar material as well as a charming small hammer (**colour plate 15**). Bone implements are mainly points or scrapers and a small group of antler points may have been used specifically for working gold into moulds (**colour plate 19**).

Finally a very common item of this period is jewellery, both beads and ornaments, in blue glass or faience. This category seems to have been exempt from the sumptuary control of the palace and is found in chamber tombs, in shrine deposits and as stray losses in settlement contexts. Simple beads are also made in various semi-precious stones (as well as in ivory and bone) and elaborate moulded ones in faience but it is the ubiquitous flat-backed mould-made glass plaques that attract particular attention. Glass which is not known in the Mediterranean area until around 1600 BC seems (on the evidence of the Ulu Burun wreck) to have been imported as a ready-made artificial 'raw' material. It was then worked into items of adornment to local design and taste. Some pieces (such as the 'beehive' beads from Room 32 of the Cult Centre on exhibit in the site museum) are of very elaborate manufacture, having been layered of two colours of glass, worked to give a wave effect and finally remoulded into the beehive shape (**colour plate 18**).

It has been argued that glass can be considered a high status product as it had to be imported but the very quantity that has been found of a material which degrades easily makes it clear that glass cannot have been subject to palatial

56 *Ivory 'candlestick' from the House of
    Shields, thirteenth century BC (54-
    449 NM 7493).*
    © Mycenae Archive: Piet de Jong

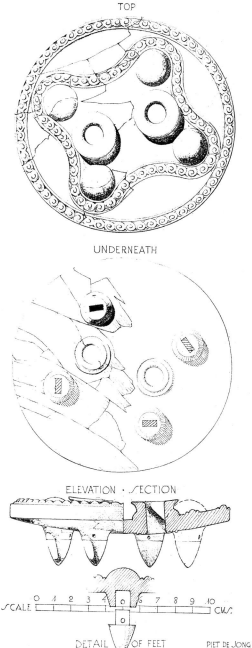

TOP

UNDERNEATH

ELEVATION · SECTION

SCALE 0 1 2 3 4 5 6 7 8 9 10 CMS.

DETAIL OF FEET   PIET DE JONG

consumption controls. It may or may not have originally been seen as a substitute
for the rare lapis lazuli but the colour was certainly important aesthetically – and
I have noted above the ornaments in terracotta coloured blue from the Tomb of
the Genii; had a shipment of glass been delayed and a substitute therefore required
in a hurry? Glass was sometimes covered in gold sheet or used in conjunction with

117

thin gold sheet to make a two colour pattern. The designs on glass are basically the same stylised patterns as are found on pottery, carefully arranged to fill the available space.

This much can be said with relative certainty but there are objects which defy interpretation. One such type is the item nicknamed 'candlestick' because of its shape but for which no explanation has as yet been put forward. It is found at Mycenae in ivory (**56**) and as a terracotta miniature and elsewhere in bronze and ivory. It will require the discovery of such an item in a primary context to solve the puzzle.

9 The economy and daily life

Engineering

We have already noted some aspects of the most outstanding accomplishments of the Mycenaeans: the tholos tombs, and the massive fortifications, but there are other examples which we can identify clearly in the landscape. One of the most obvious concerns *water management*. Water courses were given revetments at the sides in key places to prevent the sides being washed away in flash floods and the flow was softened by a series of low weirs which may also have had other uses in agriculture or even for laundry. On the other hand, the suggestion (Knauss 1996, 1997) that the Agios Giorgios bridge was in fact a dam controlling the city's water supply though intriguing cannot be accepted. At Tiryns however there is an elaborate structure to divert a water course away from the site itself; this was certainly strengthened in the Palatial period though it was probably built very much earlier in the Early Bronze Age. The other important water management scheme of the Mycenaeans is to be found Boeotia in the Copais Basin (by Orchomenos and Gla).

Skill in water management is shown too in the arrangements for drainage within the settlement. The terraces were filled with stones and the outer walls have 'weepers'. Open areas were served by a system of drains which eventually ran out through the citadel wall; all were gravity slopes but with carefully designed narrowing and special slopes to make sure that the water ran off freely but not too fast. We can tell less about arrangements for the storage of clean water. It is likely that some of the run off water was tapped for usage, as on the Cyclades today, but we have very few wells and no cisterns except the main one now approached from within the North-east Extension.

Transport and trade

Similar skills can be seen in the road network which combines several of the features already mentioned and, perhaps hardly surprisingly, anticipates the construction methods later used by the Romans; the use of the terrain, however, differs. Mycenaean roads take the form of terraces running along the contours; there are culverts and bridges to traverse the water courses. The width is nearly 12ft (3.58m), ample for both chariots and carts. Over the stone filled terrace there would have been a bedding layer of earth and over this another layer possibly of limestone chips – the suggestion of a modern road engineer but one that would have been easily available to the Mycenaeans. This network (**3, 25**) is well preserved only where it lies on the hill slopes to the north, north-east and south-east of the site. The route that must have run past Khania towards Argos can only be surmised from one crossing noted by the surveyor Steffen. It may be, however, that the good communications with the north and particularly with the fertile inland plains hidden away in the hills reflects one power base of the state. The kingdom of Agamemnon as listed in Homer certainly is centred between the Gulf of Corinth and the site of Mycenae. As well as the roads (**3**) in the immediate vicinity of the site, a trunk route connecting the Argive Plain with the Saronic Gulf and its ports has been identified; it is to this route that the Mycenaean bridge near Kazarma by the modern road to Epidaurus belongs.

One of the important results of the Mycenae Survey was to make quite clear the relationship between the many cemeteries attached to the main settlement and the road network (**25**). It must be remembered, however, that Mycenaean chamber tomb cemeteries were not notable monuments as the dromoi of the tombs would have been filled in and only marker stones visible. (The tholoi, on the other hand, would have had the dromos open to view and a handsome wall surrounding the top of the vault, where offerings might be placed.) Thus the placing of a chamber tomb group by a road may have been merely a matter of convenience rather than of display.

Evidence for land transport comes from illustrations on vases (**55**), on wall paintings and on seals as well as from terracotta miniatures (**30**). These sources tell us only of chariots, however, and it has been suggested that the chariot was little more than a status symbol or battle taxi (i.e. an armoured car rather than a tank). The chariot seems to have first been introduced in the Early Palatial period for they are well represented on the stelai of Grave Circle A (**7**) and to be of Syrian origin transmitted via Crete. The palace archives at both Knossos and Pylos however give indication of a considerable number, both serviceable and out of use. They were stored taken apart in sections and doubtless transported in the same way so they could have been carried on pack animals. The width of the roads may be aimed at chariots or at carts – but we have absolutely no evidence of any kind for carts on the mainland.

Our knowledge of *sea transport* is based on the same types of evidence supplemented by three Bronze Age wrecks which have been excavated: (in order of excavation and from east to west) Cape Gelidonya, Ulu Burun and Iria (**15**). None of these however is thought to be a Mycenaean boat, though all were involved in trade with the Mycenaean world in the hands of other nationals. Ships are generally reconstructed on the basis of terracottas and on a very clear representation on a vase from Skyros (**57**) and overall would have looked very like those on the famous Thera ship fresco (Athens, National Museum). The best evidence we have for *trade* comes from the shipwrecks. Though both Cape Gelidonya and Iria have provided important evidence, the latter particularly about connections with Cyprus, it is from Ulu Burun that we learn the most. One important point must be stressed: the bulk of the preserved cargo is of raw materials, mainly metals but also glass, woods and resins. The exotic finished items are probably the possessions of the captain or of merchants travelling with the ship.

57   *Boat shown on a stirrup jar from Skyros, twelfth century BC.*
Skyros Archaeological Museum A77

For harbours we have no tangible evidence. We assume that the ships would have been beached at night and not anchored in deeper water. Surprisingly no stone anchors, which are very prevalent in Cyprus and the Levant, have been found in Greece – perhaps itself evidence that shipping was not in the hands of the Mycenaeans themselves. The shipping routes can be guessed from information from later times and from our knowledge of currents and winds – and from the position of the wrecks!

Houses and their decoration

We have good evidence of the domestic architecture of Mycenae at this time. There are several base plans for houses which varied according to the terrain on which the house was to be built. In a flat area the plan involved a court opening onto a megaron complex whereas on sloping ground a terrace scheme was adopted with entrances at the different levels (as in some of the older houses on the steep streets of Nauplion – a comparison on which the reconstruction **colour plate 16** has been based). The rooms of this type of house were usually approached from a long corridor from which the type is named. There was always a stone foundation, either a few simple courses of walling set in a rock cut trench or a whole basement level in stone. Mud brick was used above the stone, tied into the structure with a wooden framework (**32**). Walls were coated in mud plaster very often with a lime plaster surface which could be decorated with painting. Stairs were well built, frequently in two flights supported by a central rubble pillar enclosed by wooden piers. Treads were of specially selected light stone. The core of the house was, usually, a rectangular room with central hearth approached through a columned porch – a layout known as a megaron. There seems to have been a vent above the hearth topped by a terracotta

121

chimney – a necessity to prevent rain splashing widely into the room below. Other buildings, which may have been of mixed usage like the Khania farmhouse and the buildings of the Pezoulia area, had individual plans suited to their functions.

Furnishings are little known. Several rooms and waiting areas have built benches but there seem rather surprisingly to have been no other built-in features except hearths (unlike the many built features found in the houses of the Greek islands in the last centuries). It is from illustrations particularly on seals and from terracotta miniatures that we learn of tables, chairs, footstools and perhaps beds (though more probably biers) (**30**). Mention is made of some of these in the Linear B texts. One text from Pylos records the inspection of furniture (on the occasion of the appointment of a man named Augewas as da-mo-ko-ro). This is thought to describe a storeroom rather than a suite of rooms as no beds are listed. However bedsteads are not always used and bedding is recorded on other texts. Of storage chests only the decorative components (inlays of ivory and other rich materials) remain.

Wall painting is rarely found on the walls – with a notable exception in the scenes from the Cult Centre (**colour plate 12**) now exhibited in the site museum – but fragments are widely found and a composition can often be restored by the expert, though these can reflect more of the restorer than the original. Recent excavation, particularly at Gla in Boeotia, seems to indicate that even buildings such as storerooms, kitchens and workshops could have painted decoration of this kind.

Many fragmentary pieces were found fallen in the Palace at Mycenae or removed from the walls after the earlier earthquake damage. They are of high competence but lack the naturalistic flare of many Cretan representations. The Mycenaean desire to order and schematise is less successful in the larger flatter scale of wall painting than on the demanding small fields of vase painting. Some scenes however have charm, others are of interest for the subject matter (e.g. **colour plate 10** which shows a sedan chair). In the buildings intended to impress, the walls were divided into zones: orthostats at the base imitating the stone actually used in some places, a main zone, a frieze where scenes in the miniature technique could be shown and borders (cornices etc.) with decorative motifs. Representations at Mycenae itself in the thirteenth century are typical of the mainland: hunting and battle scenes, processions, and much subsidiary decoration (spirals, triglyphs, rock work, marbling etc.) including large size figure of eight shields used in the main zone presumably instead of the actual trophies. The earliest pieces are naturalistic; those from the fourteenth century apparently rather more diverse. The inspiration of mainland wall painting certainly comes from Crete but the relation of Cretan painting itself to that of Egypt and the Levant is currently much discussed following the discovery of paintings apparently with a Minoan theme at Tell Dab'a in the Nile Delta and at Tel Kabri in Israel.

The technique employed is that of true fresco (*buon fresco*) – white lime plaster laid over a base deliberately coarsened to hold the surface layer. The colours are basic earth colours (though an intriguing and as yet unanalysed purple has now appeared at Gla). White was the background plaster for large areas but (as on pottery) details are added in a thick white paste. Some black outlining was also added after the main painting was complete. The string lines which guided the layout can on occasion be

58 Tablets inscribed in the Linear B script, thirteenth century BC.
Large page tablet from the House of the Oil Merchant, Room 1 (F0 [52-] 101 NM
7667; height 6.3in, 16cm). This room was dedicated to the storage of oil and the
tablet records the distribution of oil to named individuals.
Smaller page tablet from the House of Sphinxes, Room 4 (Go [54-] 610 NM 7708);
height 3.5in (9cm). This seems to record the non-arrival of an unknown liquid from
four named people. Note the single sign on the reverse

seen, as can the base outline in yellow-ochre (see the feet on the fresco from the
Room with the Fresco on exhibit in the site museum).

Administration

We know almost nothing about the administration of Mycenae itself; our evidence
for the bureaucratic (or 'feudal') system that prevailed and for the palace economy
which it produced comes from Knossos and Pylos where large archives of clay
tablets have been preserved. It is only an assumption, but one on which we all
work, that a similar system was in force at Mycenae, Thebes and Tiryns. In any
case the clay tablets are only preliminary administrative documents quite unlike the
clay tablets from Anatolia and the Near East. Preliminary recording of items
received or dispatched by the palace was on small clay nodules; this information
was then transferred to a thin horizontal rectangle known as a leaf tablet. Later
several of these were combined onto broader vertical rectangles known as page
tablets (**58**), on which a total might be entered too. But even so these were only
the preliminary notations of current information. Later what needed to be kept (to
allow year on year comparisons for instance) would have been transferred to
another even more perishable medium. From marks on the back of the nodules
attached to tied groups of documents at Knossos, it is suggested that parchment

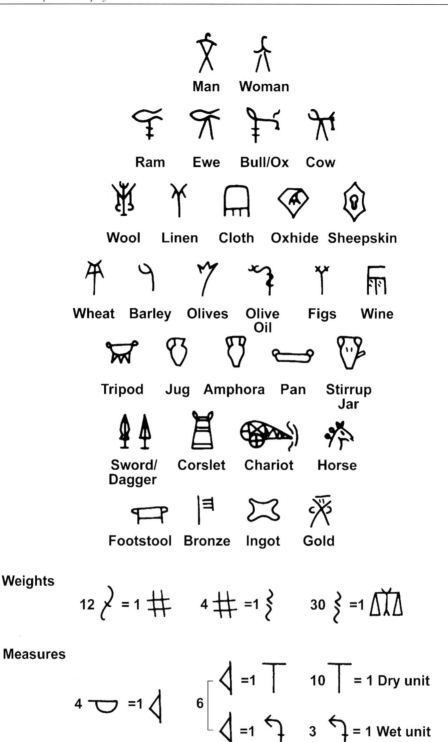

59   *Ideograms of the Linear B script*

60   *Sealings of unbaked clay inscribed in the Linear B script from the doorway to Room 1
of the House of Sphinxes, thirteenth century BC (53-501>7, NM 7632). Each
sealing is about 1in long (2.54cm). The heirloom seal of hard stone (the same was used
on each) depicts a man between two rampant wild goats and the inscriptions give names
of pots probably from deliveries to the storeroom. The sealings were preserved because
they were burnt hard in the destruction of the building*

(from sheep skin) was used. The clay tablets are of a special well-refined clay on
which the text was written with a stylus (probably of bone though none have been
securely identified). Though we call those writing the text scribes, they are
probably the actual administrators responsible for the transactions they were
recording; we can identify nearly 100 at Knossos and at least 30 at Pylos – true
scribes can be postulated only for the final stage of transfer to another medium.
The clay tablets were only sun-dried but those that have survived were fired in the
flames which destroyed the areas where they were stored. This could lead to very
uneven results: Tablet Ui 709 from Room 4 of the House of Sphinxes was found
in 1961 under the side of a large vat and the right-hand end crumbled when lifted
as it has been only partially baked.

Linear B is a syllabic script of over 100 signs representing a consonant and a
vowel. In addition there are some ideograms or rather logograms depicting individual items or products (**59** gives a selection). Most of these have been interpreted,
partly thanks to the juxtaposition of a word in the syllabary, partly from their
context. Some problems remain; we are still not sure whether the reading of the
signs taken to be wheat and barley is correct. The usual reading was adopted on
the basis of the nutritional value of the products when issued as rations but a
leading botanist suggested long ago that the actual appearance of the signs implied
the opposite and this doubt has recently been again forcefully expressed. Linear B
was deciphered as an early form of Greek by Michael Ventris in 1952 (see
Chadwick 1976 for references). It seems to be a means of writing an artificial
administrative language (a modern parallel might be the language of legal
documents). The origin of the script, which is an adaptation to Mycenaean Greek

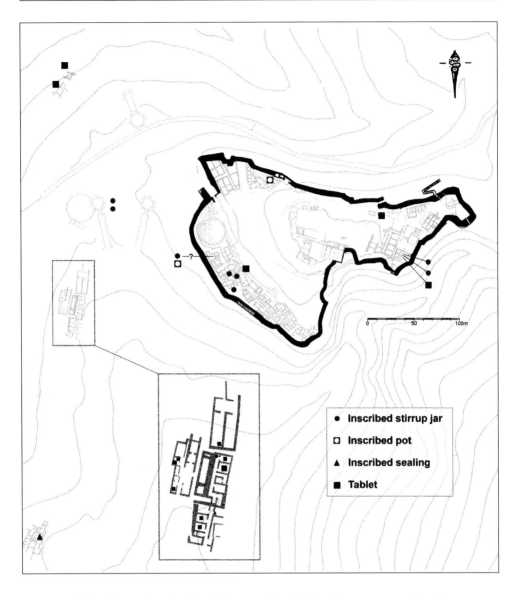

61   Citadel and town showing the find spots of inscribed tablets, pottery and sealings.
© Mycenae Archive

of the earlier Linear A script used on Crete for their non-Indoeuropean language, is not clear. The script certainly dates from the Early Palatial period on the mainland but is likely to have been developed at Knossos in the late fifteenth century (Late Minoan II) when Mycenaeans, possibly a group of warriors, seem to have had considerable influence there. It would only have taken one enterprising bi- or multi-lingual merchant/administrator, perhaps one with knowledge of how scripts were used in the Near East – Driessen (1992) calls him a literary Daidalos

– to make this innovation. Such an international basis for the weight system has been suggested.

The texts that survive from Mycenae were not found in the Palace but in what appear to have been commercial complexes scattered all over the site (**61**) and under palatial control. Of great importance was the find in 2000 of a tablet from Petsas' House which can be firmly dated to the later fourteenth century. With its certain early context this tablet is at present unique on the mainland but serves to help bridge the gap, which has caused much unease, between the similar texts from Knossos (early fourteenth century) and those from elsewhere (mainly thirteenth century).

A number of words on the tablets from Pylos are administrative titles or the names of social classes. The meanings of these are often identified from classical Greek usage checked against the contexts in which they are used. The *wanaks* would be identifiable as a personage of major importance even if the word were not continued into classic Greek as -*anax*- king. The word, which is never coupled with a personal name, appears in some contexts to be a divine title. He does, however, have intriguing privileges and attributes: a royal domain, royal garments often of royal purple, personnel appointed by him and exemption from some taxes. The other classical word for king – *basileus* – also occurs but has a much reduced status being only a chief or leader of a group (even of smiths). An echo of this can be found in Homer where the chieftains of Ithaca are referred by this term. Next to the *wanaks* in seniority came the *lawagetas* who at Pylos controlled an estate one third the size of that of the *wanaks*. The term *damos* is also used and much recent work has concentrated on defining exactly what is meant by this word, so over-shadowed by its later meaning.

The position of women in the texts is a good example of the narrow range that the records cover. Women appear in only two functions: religious personnel and female workers, most of whom seem to be slaves or tied workers. The latter comprise textile workers, corn grinders, water carriers, waitresses and 'maids of all work'. Many of these women have children listed with them and some are described as from places in the Eastern Aegean (Miletus, Cnidos, Lemnos, Chios) presumably where they were captured or bought. The list of male occupations is much more extensive and includes masons and smiths but no farmers and few potters.

Overall the picture of Mycenaean society given by the tablets is of a redistribu-tive economy with very strong central control. The manufacturing process was tightly controlled with targets set and all transactions recorded in detail. The result of this is that we have a very broad picture of the areas of the economy which the palace controlled and little or no information about other matters. We have direct evidence for the contribution to the palace of: grain, olive oil, other food stuffs like honey, condiments (spices and products like saffron, coriander and cyperus), metals, hides, textiles (also raw wool and flax), goats (and horns), wood. Industrial type production includes textiles, bronze working, manufacture of chariots and other weapons, prepa-ration of perfumed oil, furniture, and leather working. But there is no word for farmer or any actual agricultural worker, no merchants or traders. The absence from the texts of agricultural produce which has actually been found in excavations, such as legumes and millet (though this is confined to the north of Greece) again demon-strates the bias of the documentary evidence.

Another area where it is difficult to reconcile the texts with the archaeological evidence concerns weight systems. We can work out the various proportions from the texts (**59**) but linking this to the weights of the actual pieces recovered is not yet possible. Various suggestions for the basic weight system have been made, deriving it from either or both the Egyptian and the Babylonian systems. Recent work suggests that there may have been a change during the later Palatial period.

Cloth, clothing and personal adornment

Key 'invisibles' of the Mycenaean economy are *textiles*. The product does not survive but from the Linear B texts, from iconographic evidence (wall painting, seals etc.) and from ethnographic information we can make suggestions. Though an excellent reconstruction of the management of flocks for the production of wool, based on the Linear B texts from Knossos combined with information of the medieval wool trade in England, was presented over 40 years ago by John Killen it is only now that a real attempt is being made to use ethnographic information to elucidate the texts for the next stage of the process: the actual textiles. Until now there has been far too much supposition by those who have little or no knowledge of the various types of textile and how they are made.

For Mycenae (and indeed for much of mainland Greece) there is one major diffi-culty about textile production: the scarcity of loomweights. From Mycenae itself there is a small group of clay loomweights of the type known from Crete from below the floor of the 'Guardroom' of the Palace but no others from anywhere on the site, nor of stones which show marks from being used in this way. At present it would seem that textile production was an industrial activity which was carried out in specialist workshops in areas as yet unexcavated. It must, moreover, be remembered how restricted our evidence is for both ordinary houses and for specialist buildings around the acropolis at Mycenae. What were once regularly identified as 'spindle whorls' now called *conuli* have been discussed above (p.113)

The Linear B ideogram for cloth (**59**) seems to represent a piece on a loom with hanging warps or a dress-length with warp threads still hanging from it. A variant shows what may be decoration on the cloth. Wool is the main product, but linen was made as well. There may have been some wild silk but cotton was not yet used. At Knossos the whole system is organised by one man and all stages are carefully recorded. Pylos tells us of the women workers while at Mycenae we learn of recipi-ents. The technical terms in the Linear B texts have been interpreted, as often, by their derivatives in classical Greek. Many make good sense to all, but other features which have puzzled the linguists are of no surprise to those acquainted with the ethnographic background. The women within the palace at Knossos who add extra high class finish may be embroiderers working on a base cloth made elsewhere; the headband weavers are surely braidweavers producing trimmings for human dress (both male and female)

62 *Suggested types of male and female clothing*

as well as horse trappings and bindings; gifts to gods and men of finished garments or of dress-lengths have ample parallels in classical, medieval and later times. Above all the vast array of weaving techniques available even in a simple society and the basic distinction between weaving and embroidery must be remembered.

The clothing of the Mycenaeans (**62**) is now better understood thanks largely to wall painting. Diana Wardle (1997) gives an excellent up-to-date summary. On the mainland male dress is basically a tunic edged with braid which can be worn on its own, under armour or made warmer or smarter by the addition of a cloak. A decorated kilt seems to be male dress wear and is produced and worn similarly to the overskirt of women. The painted representations of women that survive seem all to be of them wearing their 'Sunday best', but from figurines (**29**) we may suggest that again we have a simple basic garment, though long not short. This was belted, perhaps giving a blouson effect and sometimes high under the breasts. Over it could be added a jacket and a flounced wrap-around skirt. Figurines and the ivory trio from the Mycenae citadel (**43 & 44**) also show a knitted or crocheted shawl. Both fabric and knitted shawls form a very useful part of female dress in many societies and can be used by a mother to carry a baby. The breasts in representations in all media are almost always shown quite distinctly even when clearly covered and it is therefore likely that none of the representations depict actual bare breasts. The presence of small nipples on some of the figures from the Cult Centre (**45**) led to the idea that they were hermaphrodites but as nipples are also shown on one of the clearly male figures from Phylakopi, the presence of nipples may be considered as nothing more momentous than realism.

It is a rather surprising fact that the Mycenaeans did not in fact illustrate their monarchs or other leaders. The people shown on wall paintings are not individuals but almost certainly types as are representations in other materials (**45 & 46**). This caused some difficulty when we were asked to suggest hairstyles for the Manchester reconstructions (**6**) particularly for the men. A single amethyst gem comes from Grave Circle B (grave Gamma) showing a male head with long hair, flowing beard, fringe and distinctive forelock. But this is a Cretan gem, though the sketch drawn on the back of one of the tablets from the House of the Oil Merchant does seem to have the same features. Almost the only clear representation from the thirteenth century is the ivory head (**colour plate 13**) which shows short hair at the back with long forelocks neatly parted and combed back behind the ears, the whole held down by a fillet. Women's styles can be suggested both from wall painting and from figurines. At the front there is a fringe, sometimes rendered as stiff curls, and at the back a long plait or twist starting on the crown of the head. In elaborate versions there are three (or more) plaits and sometimes curls at the sides of the face (giving the effect of sideburns on figurines). On a painting from Akrotiri the women seem to have a close-knit net over the head through which the plait descends.

Wall painting too is the main source for information on personal adornment and jewellery though there are some actual finds like the hairpins from a tomb at Pylos. Necklaces of various kinds are widely worn and shown even on figurines. Earrings and a hair decoration which can be paralleled in Grave III of Grave Circle A are worn by one of the women on a painting at Akrotiri (these are contemporary) but are not known after this either in paintings or as finds. Gems or signets were worn on the wrist as well as in rings but again these are mainly characteristic of the Early Palatial period though we know that signets remained in use throughout the Palatial period.

Diet

Study of food and drink has advanced greatly in the last five years under the co-ordination of the Minoan-Mycenaean Food and Drink Project with its excellent exhibition in Athens in 1999 (Tzedakis & Martlew 1999). Environmental material had

Fish

Meat

Honey & Nuts

Fruit & Vegetables

Dairy Products

Grapes & Olives

Cereals & Pulses

63 *Suggested diet of the Bronze Age showing the proportions of the different types of food-stuffs.* © Mycenae Archive

been kept and recorded by several of the early excavators and the evidence from it was well summarised in the 1930s by Vickery. The interest was revived in the late 1960s and 1970s with the development of various new retrieval techniques but reached something of a dead end. The recent application of organic residue analysis, of DNA testing and a new look at the actual remains and the documentary evidence have produced intriguing results.

Food would have been similar to a basic Mediterranean diet (**63**) but without the ubiquitous tomato and other vegetables and fruits which were introduced from the New World in the Middle Ages. Rations at Mycenae consisted of grain (wheat or barley), olives and wine with the addition in some texts of figs and of flavourings. Excavation (of two deposits) at Mycenae has yielded Emmer and Einkorn wheat, barley, bitter vetch, lentils, fava beans and a few grass peas. All three grains are most likely to have been used as the base for a porridge (to be eaten from a Deep Bowl **28**) though Emmer Wheat can be roasted and mixed with things like nuts to make a 'snack food' that could be carried with one when away from home. Barley can also be used as a thickener for soups and stews or as the basis of beer. The fava beans could also have been used in stews or perhaps as a Bronze Age version of the popular modern meze. It is likely that these basic dishes were both supplemented nutritionally and made more attractive by the addition of flavourings like onion and the range of wild herbs still popular in Greece today. The list of flavourings on the so-called 'Spice' tablets from the House of Sphinxes includes cardamom, celery, fennel, mint, safflower and sesame. Not only would a range of condiments like these add flavour to the rather bland stews but, as Hillman has pointed out, several of them would be of considerable value in reducing the flatulence which a basic diet of that kind would otherwise cause. The Linear B texts indicate that a day's ration of cereals was three of the smallest measure 'Z'. This measure is represented by a logogram resembling the handle-less cup (**54, 59**). On the mainland the largest of these cups measures half a pint (300ml – similar to the culinary cup measure as used in Great Britain), a suitable size for a single helping of this type of food.

The *livestock* documented from excavation include much sheep/goat as well as some cattle and varying amounts of pig. Among wild animals there are deer, boar and hare. Retrieval methods suitable for the recovery of fish bones have not been in use but marine shells are relatively common. As we have seen recent S.I.A. studies seems to show that only some of the elite enjoyed marine foods in their diet. In addition animals give secondary products like milk, cheese and yoghurt which can be enjoyed without slaughtering the beast (which is of value alive also for its wool). It must be remembered, when consulting the published diet information, that in DNA testing these secondary products give the same result as the actual animal. The use of juvenile pig in religious feasting is just beginning to emerge from current bone studies.

The results of the organic residue analyses from cooking vessels at Mycenae suit the archaeological evidence well. Two pots had contained a stew with olive oil, meat and lentils and one a mixture of olive oil, wine and fish. Wine including a resinated version had been stored in many vessels, including a Canaanite amphora (**50**) from the Levant. From Thebes a deep bowl, the 'porridge bowl' shape, had contained a cereal or pulses. There is also evidence on the mainland for fermented beverages from barley and from honey which seem on occasion to have been mixed with wine as well into an elaborate 'mull' which sounds disgusting but which the scientist concerned assures us is very nice to drink.

Religion

The sources for our assessment of Mycenaean religion are the same three that have been valid for so many aspects: archaeological evidence, iconography and the Linear B texts. There is an overall problem about how much of the Minoan cult paraphernalia which are depicted or have been found has the same meanings in the Mycenaean cult as it does in Crete. The divergence is just as true of the thirteenth century as it was of the remains from the sanctuary of Apollo Maleatis in the fifteenth.

The cult buildings identified at Mycenae are small in area but three of the four contained functional features and dedications. Shrine Gamma in its early phase had an unusual altar from which a covered channel ran to a cooking vessel imbedded by the adjacent wall. After this was covered a small structure was constructed outside the entrance to the room which is assumed to have taken over the function of an altar. The 'Temple' had a central altar, a series of stepped benches on which one figure and a small portable altar were displayed. In two areas (the sealed Room 19 and the adjacent alcove) was a mass of dedications: figures, pottery, single items of jewellery and three large portable altars. One of the portable altars but neither of the built ones showed marks of burning. In the Room with the Fresco there was a central horse-shoe-shaped hearth, a high bench or altar on which were displayed valuable items including the male ivory head (**colour plate 13**), perhaps a deity, and a plain clay bath tub. Quantities of pottery and many conuli came from the deposit in the room. Immediately behind this room, another small room seems to have served as both shrine and store. Here in the inner corner, not visible from outside the room, there stood on a low dais a small figure with in front of her the remains of an elaborate pectoral of glass beads (**colour plate 18**). The deposit in the room included much pottery, many conuli and many ivories, both fully and partially worked. Two features should be noted. First this complex is linked to, but is not an immediate part of, the Palace and at Mycenae (unlike Pylos) we have no evidence to suggest whether or not the Megaron of the Palace was used for religious purposes. Second the Cult Centre comprises several shrines differing widely from one another in their attributes suggesting, as do the texts, a variety of independent deities. The more or less contemporary complex at Phylakopi on Melos is similar and there is a striking parallel to the many obscure but venerated cults later found on the Athenian Acropolis.

Wall painting shows that processions played a key role in cult practice. The best preserved examples come from Thebes and from Tiryns (Athens, National Museum) but fragments of a similar composition were identified by Mark Cameron from the area of the Cult Centre at Mycenae. The construction of what Mylonas has labelled the 'Processional Way' leading apparently from the Grand Staircase of the Palace to the Cult Centre, as well as the other approach passages and walkways, argues for this practice. The only wall painting published from this Processional Way, though very fragmentary, shows, not people walking with offerings as in other compositions, but a chariot proceeding toward the Centre. There seems to be evidence that not only were future offerings displayed in such processions but also the riches of the shrine and symbols of the deities. A text from Pylos (TN 316) lists an inventory of gold vessels which it has been suggested represent a processional display, and paintings both from near the Cult Centre at Mycenae and from Tiryns show figurines held in the hand. It would have been possible to carry each of the figures found in the various parts of the Cult Centre in this way. The overall effect of such processions would have been that shown in small scale on gold signets (though these are of the Early Palatial period). As cult buildings themselves were small, the emphasis on procession would have allowed much greater participation. The whole might well have resembled the procession on the eve of a Saint's day in Greece today. On its route up to the Palace the Processional Way would have passed near the Rhyton Well where several broken items of cultic significance were found, giving the well its name. These fragments may relate to the theory recently proposed that some items of cult paraphernalia were deliberately broken after ceremonies.

What the actual offerings were is difficult to ascertain. The iconographic representations show containers, particularly jugs and boxes both of which may have been offered for themselves or their contents. The texts list as offerings oil (usually perfumed), oxen, sheep, goats, pigs, grain, wine, honey, unguent, wool and cloth. Oil, honey, grain and wool are the most common. It is not clear, however, how and why these were offered: whether for use by the temple staff or as a source of potential income. Recently found texts from Thebes mention food stuffs in such small quantities that they are assumed to be religious offerings.

Other texts, however, from both Thebes and Pylos seem to deal with provisions for religious festivals with large quantities of foodstuffs including various animals. There is at present no evidence of any kind from the Mycenaean world of actual burnt sacrifices – whole animals consumed by flame – though the offering of specific parts of a sacrificed animal to the deity (as in Homer) seems quite likely. The main part of the beast would have been eaten by the participants. Similarly with wine, the number of drinking cups has suggested libations but they could just as well represent actual drinking or a combination with a libation or toast followed by consumption. The discovery at the recently excavated sanctuary on Methana of the burnt bones of young pig in the cult room has led to the detailed examination (still in progress) of the animal bones from the British section of the excavation of the Cult Centre at Mycenae. There seems to be some comparable evidence for the presence of young pig though here we have no primary bone deposits (one was found by Mylonas in the courtyard area but this has not yet been studied). There is also an unusually high proportion of doves of various species, which bring to mind the presence of this motif on seals, although they may well have been offerings for sacrifice as with other religions.

10 The Post-Palatial period

The devastation which occurred at Mycenae and apparently other sites at the end of the thirteenth century brought to an end the Palatial period. The bureaucratic administration which had been fully stretched to deal with the expansion of the first half of the century followed so soon by a devastating earthquake was not able to cope with another disaster on this scale. But it is not so much the disasters themselves but the cumulative effect of them on an overstretched economy that may indeed have already been suffering from a diminution of trade or a lack of the raw materials sought in trade. This phenomenon, which gives us the Aristotelian definition of the tragic hero, is known as catastrophe theory and we can see in our own times how the demise of an overpowering bureaucracy such as that in the Soviet Union can trigger both social and economic disruption quite out of proportion to the actual event which overturned the bureaucracy – and which indeed may be such as to leave no trace in the archaeological record. The widespread drought which is documented in the texts of the Near East at this period and which seems to have contributed heavily to the downfall of the Hittite Empire may also have affected Greece but we have no evidence of this at present.

At Mycenae itself the basic devastation seems to have been largely the result of widespread fires in many but not all areas of the citadel. At other centres there seems to be more evidence of earthquake and the Mycenae fires may be the result of an earthquake.

The excavation of the Citadel House Area demonstrated the effect of this fire most dramatically. The burning of the wood and mudbrick structures when combined with fallen stone foundations gave the debris a consistency almost of concrete. Heavy rains on the surface of this then spread the resulting slurry over wide areas sloping down over this whole part of the site. The devastation was too great for immediate extensive rebuilding.

After a short time, however, some of the debris was shifted, but not removed, to form a series of heavy terraces at a much higher level. Several pre-existing walls had remained standing, where sufficiently well built, and these were reused. Crucial to the whole enterprise was the use of the citadel wall as a supporting wall for the terraces. Another disaster, and one that again left copious material on the floors, followed. As this was marked in the Citadel House Area by the collapse of a stout wall surviving from the Palatial period it may be that this was yet another earthquake. Modern village expectation in the vulnerable regions of Greece is for a major earthquake every 20 years. After some rebuilding and occupation over a fairly short period, this section of the site was abandoned. There was no serious rebuilding here for a long time and the area adjacent to the citadel wall was covered with layers of wash containing the

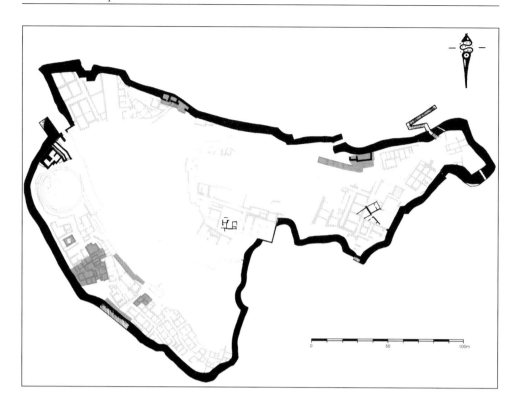

64   Plan of the Citadel to show the areas where we have definite evidence of Post-Palatial
     occupation. © Mycenae Archive

handsome pottery (**66 & 67**) that marks the late twelfth century. Good stratigraphy of
this period was also recovered by Mylonas in similar layers against the east (Mycenaean)
face of the Hellenistic tower. There is similar rebuilding too over the Processional Way
and the east part of House A of the South-west Quarter (**64**).

There are two problems of interpretation that face the excavators at Mycenae: to
what extent is this scenario repeated in other parts of the site and if the sherd
evidence is slight and there are no restorable pots can we be sure of the date of
construction/occupation/destruction. In addition there is an enigma: where were
the buildings in which were used these handsome pots found in quantity by the
citadel wall at the west?

For the central palace area there is absolutely no hard evidence of what happened
but the presence of structures immediately over the destruction debris in the Great
Court suggests reoccupation. The recent confirmation that the building within the
Megaron at Tiryns was built in the twelfth century leads me to suggest that the
Mycenae structures too are of this date. Rodenwaldt, who had seen both, compared
the masonry at Mycenae to that of the Tiryns building, and Dörpfeld's plan of the
palace area (**65**) published by Tsountas shows a well laid out building of some sophis-
tication and only of poor quality in relation to the palace beneath it. A photograph

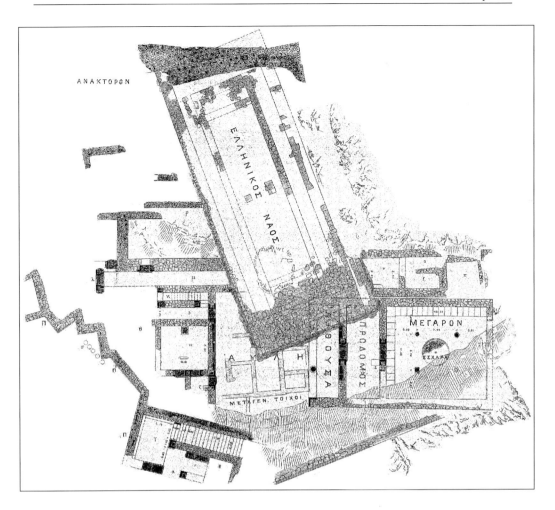

65 *Plan of the Palace showing the later structure over the Great Court which is now suggested to be the Palace (VI) of the twelfth century BC. Plan made by the German archaeologist Dörpfeld for Tsountas and published in the Praktika of the Archaeological Society for 1898. The terrace of the later (Archaic and Hellenistic) temples is also shown*

probably dating from Rodenwaldt's work in 1914 (Klein 1997) shows part of these structures nestling within the area of the Great Court. They have always been considered to be Geometric because Tsountas with sad hindsight recorded:

> In the excavation daybook before I realised what if any relationship there was between the different walls, of which only the upper sections had been cleared, I noted that the deposit between these walls which subsequently proved to be of later date there were found some pieces of vases of *geometric type* [his italics] with designs of animals and birds, but in the lower burnt layers and where there were no later walls all the finds were of the Mycenaean style.

66   Large jar, possibly a grave marker, decorated with birds and horses, late twelfth century BC (64-564 MM 29160; height 18.5in, 47.5cm). © Mycenae Archive: W.D. Taylour

It is not clear whether in 1886 he means true 'Geometric' or possibly LH IIIC Middle with its handsome birds and animals (**66 & 67**). When the structures over the Great Court were taken down in 1920 no sherds later than LH III were found as would be expected if reconstruction was carried out immediately on top of the destruction debris as in the Citadel House Area.

There is also reoccupation of similar type within the House of Columns. Here a simple building was constructed at an angle over the western of the two megara. Other areas where clear evidence of twelfth-century occupation has been found (**64**) are largely on the north side of the acropolis: the Granary (see above p.79), the fortification wall north of House M and a new roadway over the North Storerooms with a building beside it to the north by the citadel wall.

The difficulties with the evidence result mainly from the actions of those building the Hellenistic township who dug down in the debris to find solid foundations for their new buildings but also from the extent of early excavations before, as we have seen, knowledge of the pottery sequence allowed running interpretation of the strata as they were cleared. In addition to the problems of the Palace the situation can be well illustrated by our attempts to identify the function of the

67 *Pottery of the Post Palatial period.* © Mycenae Archive.
   *1. Simple deep bowl; 2. Deep bowl in the Close style; 3. Amphora; 4. Stirrup jar in
   the Close style; 5. Krater in the Close style*

Warrior Vase (**colour plate 20**). This large polychrome krater dating stylistically from the second half of the twelfth century was found by Schliemann at a depth of 5m (presumably from the pre-existing surface) in the area of the House named from it the House of the Warrior Vase. The depth might signify that the vase was in the main occupation levels of the house but comparison with the stratigraphy to the south makes it more likely – but quite impossible to prove – that it, like the large jar (**66**), comes from the reoccupation or wash levels above the houses of the Palatial period and might even be a grave marker of some kind.

 This period has been called 'a city society' in contrast to the palatial of the previous centuries. It starts with a long slow but steady recuperation from the disasters marked by economic prudence and it is clear that there must have been some kind of governance. At Mycenae we do not have the evidence for a large settlement of this period outside the walls as we do at Tiryns but the continued use of a large proportion of the chamber tomb cemeteries indicates a reasonable population level. At present it seems likely that it is only the third disaster mentioned above that may have driven some of the population overseas. There they found areas which had also been devastated from a variety of causes where over time they established themselves and continued to produce pottery in the same simple styles they had developed on the mainland. They kept in contact with home, however, and the elaborate florid pottery style which marks the middle phase of this period is prevalent both on the mainland, in the islands and in the Eastern Mediterranean. It does not penetrate to the north where the simpler style continues over several centuries.

 Some new features occur during this middle phase. One is the most startling new discovery of recent years at Mycenae. At Khania about one and a half miles (2.5km) to the south-west of the citadel and directly on the ancient road to Argos lies an unusual burial site (**colour plate 21**). It is a low tumulus or cremation platform, surrounded by a row of orthostats, into which was laid a series of burials in simple pots. This structure is at present unparalleled at this period.

 The end of the period is marked by a severe decline in the decorative and sometimes the actual quality of the pottery. The unpainted wares from the East Basement of the Granary are particularly and surprisingly ill-made. The fires that destoyed the Granary and the other buildings do not mark the absolute end of the Mycenaean period. Occupation continues probably into the full Iron Age without an actual break but at a very low level both of size and wealth.

11 Later Mycenae

[See plan **68** throughout]

The situation for which we have evidence at the end of the Bronze Age continues
without a break into the Early Iron Age. Slim strata of wash with pottery of
Submycenaean type exist in the higher levels of the Citadel House Area, and a series
of graves of the phase that straddles the Submycenaean/Protogeometric periods is
dug into the slope of the debris over the west slope of the site. Other graves of
similar date are known in the Prehistoric Cemetery area and over the Ivory and
Panagia Houses. Though there are no structural remains, steady simple occupation
is clearly present.

Settlement traces (mainly pot scatters but some actual structures by the Ivory
Houses) and graves of the *Geometric* period are widely found both inside and outside
the walls. Recent excavation in the Pezoulia area gives evidence of agricultural
exploitation. But it is the problems of cult, the proliferation of small sanctuaries and
particularly whether the finds of Iron Age material near or in tholos and chamber
tombs mean that a 'hero cult' was practised here, which are of greater impact. The
recent assessments (Antonaccio 1995) have seen the interpretation of hero cult
gradually diminishing from widespread cult in Bronze Age tombs to a more
pragmatic approach in which placatory offerings were made when a tomb was acci-
dentally discovered. The number of sanctuaries in comparison with the settlement
evidence is most surprising. Is this to some extent a reflection of the past importance
of Mycenae to the inhabitants of the district as a whole? It is certainly not clear
whether the spread of the Homeric poems is the cause or the result of a growing
consciousness of an heroic past. It is however clear that it was around the middle of
the eighth century BC that sanctuaries were founded beside the roads running north
and south from the site. A small Geometric shrine has been excavated at the south-
east end of the Koutsoumbela ridge but is not yet published. This lies near a recent
route that may also have been used in Mycenaean times. Somewhat similar in
position though nearer to the acropolis is what may be an apsidal shrine identified
by Verdelis east of the Ivory Houses on the road south from the site. The earliest
dedications published both from the Enyalios sanctuary and the Shrine by the Bridge
(often loosely called the Agamemnoneion) are of Geometric date. The former lies
beside roadway M3 and the latter and the sanctuary by the Ivory Houses by M4.
There are also enigmatic circular platforms just south of Grave Circle B though
perhaps these are connected to the wall surrounding the Tomb of Clytemnestra
rather than the much earlier structure.

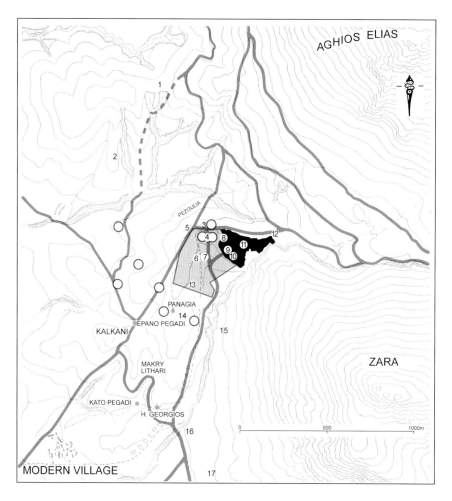

68   *The Area of Mycenae showing the monuments of the First Millennium BC.*
© Mycenae Archive.

*1. Shrine of Enalyios; 2. Geometric shrine on the Koutsoumbela ridge; 3. Perseia Fountain House; 4. Hellenistic Theatre; 5. Hellenistic Houses on Mycenaean foundations; 6. Graves, Geometric and Hellenisitic; 7. Structures and ?shrine within/over Mycenaean chamber tomb; 8. Hellenistic polygonal rebuilding in the Lion Gate Bastion; 9. Citadel House Area (see plan **74**); 10. Hellenistic tower; 11. Temple: Archaic and Hellenistic; 12. Hellenistic polygonal rebuilding at the north-east corner of the Citadel; 13. Hellenistic town wall; 14. Archaic dedications at the Treasury of Atreus; 15. Archaic tombs; 16. Shrine by the Bridge (the 'Agamemnoneion'); 17. Archaic tombs at Tzerania*

The dedications continue at the Shrine by the Bridge into the fifth century, probably beyond the disablement of the walls by the Argives in 468 BC. Whether this shrine was at this time dedicated to Agamemnon has been the subject of discussion. Two of the possible inscriptions come from below the Hellenistic terracing but are of uncertain date themselves.

69 *Krater of the Archaic period from beside the wall, faced with poros blocks, surrounding the dome of the Treasury of Atreus (55-701 MM 9083; diameter 10.25in, 26cm). The vase is decorated on this side with a running horse in dark paint and an unexplained symbol in white paint.* © Mycenae Archive: Piet de Jong

Even if we reassign the structures within the palace court there is considerable material (both pottery and small finds) of Protogeometric and Geometric date from the summit of the acropolis. Klein (1997, 316) suggests the establishment of cult on the later temple site 'from the Geometric period onwards' (i.e. the ninth century BC) and the Protogeometric pottery in this otherwise unlikely spot might be taken to indicate an even earlier start. Once again there is discussion about the deity worshipped here. A bronze plaque found by Tsountas on the acropolis, though not on the temple site, mentions Athena but restudy of the evidence (summarised Klein 1997, 297-8) now suggests that it is Hera who was the deity worshipped here.

For the *Archaic* period there is no actual settlement evidence but the recent discovery of tombs at two points along the road to the Heraion (M4) would suggest occupation. This may be indicated too by a pair of inscriptions found near the Perseia Fountain House which mention officials of the cult of Perseus acting as referees in disputes arising from ritual contests by boys. The main part of the inscription is dated to the late sixth century and an addendum on the capital which crowned it to the early fifth century. It is suggested that the boys completed in gorgon masks like those from Tiryns exhibited in Nauplion. There are other indications of cult activity. From beside the enclosure wall of the mound over the Treasury of Atreus came a seventh-century dedicatory krater with the representation of a horse on one side (**69**) and a bird on the other. This type is rare but this example compares with pieces from Tiryns

70 *Head of ?Hera as a bride
in the Dedalic style from
the Temple of the Archaic
period (NM 2869; height
(as drawn without border)
12.5in, 31.5cm).*
© Mycenae Archive

and from a small shrine at Kourtaki in the Argive plain. The shrine on the top of the acropolis acquires built form in this period. Klein's recent detailed study suggests a date in the last quarter of the seventh century for a temple of innovative design related to developments in the Corinthia, notably at Isthmia. It was not a peripteral Doric temple but had other innovative features including sculptural decoration on the south face (presumably the entrance). The three best pieces of the eight that survive are exhibited in Room 7 of the National Museum in Athens. These show the veiled bust of a female in an advanced Daedalic style (**70**), a man being grasped by wild beasts, and a helmeted warrior. Other fragments not exhibited show sections of four further figures and part of the edging of a relief block with a long slanted object, possibly the limb of an animal. The reliefs are of two different types of stone, at two different scales and have two different styles of framing. The likelihood is that they formed a frieze of individual edged scenes either as a socle or higher on the wall of a small building. The female figure could well be Hera herself in the pose of a bride but no suggestion has been made for the subject matter of the frieze as a whole.

This emphasis on Hera links to the suggestion made by Hall (1995) that Mycenae had control of the Argive Heraion at this period and that this formed part of the fatal rivalry with Argos itself. Certainly all the archaeological evidence shows that the actual road, the physical link to the Heraion, was in use and well maintained at this period.

Classical period: we know from Herodotus that the contingent sent by Mycenae and Tiryns to the battle of Platea numbered 400. The name of the site is recorded on the serpent column set up at Delphi later as a memorial (**71**). According to Diodorus (ix.65) the Argives destroyed Mycenae in 468 BC after a siege with their allies from Tegea and Kleonai as the result of a quarrel about the administration of the Argive Heraion and the Nemean Games. Pausanias' explanation was simply that the Argives were jealous of the courage of Mycenae at Thermopylae and Platea. He also says that the Argives did not actually take Mycenae because of the strength of the walls but the Mycenaeans were forced to abandon the city from lack of provisions. This would perhaps explain the action of the Argives in disabling the walls.

The destruction at Mycenae was selective but probably included the temple. The fortification walls were not razed to the ground but rendered useless by the destruction of key sections, notably the three main strong points: by the Lion Gate and Grave Circle A, the possible West Gate and the lookout to the northeast. There is a problem whether any of the dedications at the various shrines can be dated after 468 BC, as this date has been used circularly to give a date to pottery styles of the period. The sherd from over Grave Circle A which bears the inscription 'To the hero' has already been mentioned. Publication of the new tomb material may help.

Mycenae may have been rendered impotent by the Argives at this time but it remained well known in literature. Though Aeschylus sets the Agamemnon in Argos (apparently for political expediency), much of the physical description suits Mycenae much better. Both Sophocles and Euripides set their tragedies in Mycenae. Schliemann was so impressed by the detail in Euripides that he thought the dramatist must have

71 *Serpent Column erected at Delphi to celebrate the Greek victory at Platea over the Persians in 479 BC. This was removed to Constantinople by the Emperor Constantine and later placed in the Hippodrome where it was turned into a fountain. The lowest section still survives. The names of the Greek cities, including Mycenae, participating in the battle were engraved on the column; the tripod vessel at the top was of gold. The Column was originally about 23ft (7m) tall without the tripod. After sketch by the French excavators at Delphi:*
© Mycenae Archive

72   *Perseia Fountain House of the Hellenistic period from the west.*
Mycenae Archive: © V&N Tombazi 1952

visited the site. Thucydides (1,9,1) was also well aware of the importance of the site and its monarch. This situation continued through the fourth century.

Early in the third century, however, in the *Hellenistic period* the Argives had a change of heart (brought on no doubt by military necessity) and established at Mycenae a *koma*, a fortified outpost on their northern frontier. Thanks to inscriptions (few but most informative), historical references in Plutarch and Livy, and the actual archaeological remains, we know a lot about this 'village'.

The initial establishment involved the restoration of the walls and the enclosure of an area outside them, the building of a temple on the summit, the foundation of a fountain house and a theatre. Most of the citadel was occupied by housing

73   Hellenistic Theatre overlying the Tholos Tomb of Clytemnestra.
© Mycenae Archive: Alan Wace 1950

(including numerous cisterns) as well as the lower town within and outside the new town wall (**68**). The gaps in the walls were filled with limestone masonry in a handsome polygonal technique which can be seen by the visitor most easily in the curved section within the Lion Gate bastion. For the temple it was necessary to extend and strengthen the terrace on which the Archaic temple had stood. From the foundations it can be seen that this was again non-peripteral with a simple *sekos* lying north to south, probably with an altar on the level below which would have been approached along the terrace overlying the Mycenaean approach from the north-west. Almost none of the architectural members of the temple remain; it is possible that the well-cut poros blocks were deliberately removed by the Venetians in 1700 in their search for stone for building the Palamede fortress at Nauplion. Scattered capitals and column shafts from around the site show that other structures had architectural decoration. The Perseia Fountain House (**72**) (once identified as a gymnasium) but completely excavated in the 1950s stood beside the approach to the Lion Gate. The theatre (**73**) lay over the dromos of the Tomb of Clytemnestra and used the slope to back the *cavea*. Only the bottom row of seats was of stone and they have suffered badly in recent years from the pathway by which tourists visit the tholos. Publication of the scattered evidence for this monument is in progress. Though Hellenistic houses overlay almost all the Mycenaean remains on the acropolis and still form, in certain areas notably the slope at the west between

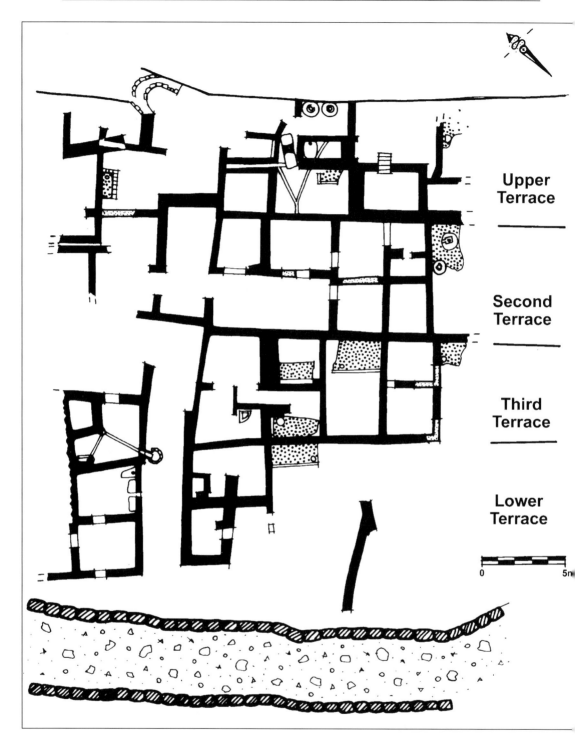

Upper
Terrace

Second
Terrace

Third
Terrace

Lower
Terrace

74   *Hellenistic houses overlying the Citadel House Area.* © Mycenae Archive

the top of the Great Ramp and the Palace, a conspicuous part of the visible remains, little attention was paid to them by the first excavators and material from them only kept sporadically. In the Citadel House Area, though the Hellenistic levels had to be removed in order to excavate below them, it was possible to make detailed plans (**74**). The result is of considerable interest. The houses lay in neat rows in three carefully built terraces and an open one below to the west. The features of the houses, which in each case include a washing area and a large number of loomweights, led to the interpretation of the area as a dye-works. However these features are common to Hellenistic housing throughout Greece. Each house did have a bath/laundry and weaving was carried out by the women (presumably) of the house at home on the vertical looms which require loomweights (a striking contrast to the Mycenaean period; see p.128).

Thanks to the inscriptions found on the site and information from another similar *koma* at Asine and from Argos itself, Boethius was able in the excavation report in BSA XXV to give a vivid description of the organisation of the settlement and its relations to Argos. We know too from other sources of Mycenae's involvement in two episodes of Hellenistic history. In 235 BC the Argive tyrant Aristippos was killed here as he fled homewards after an unsuccessful assault on Kleonai – and perhaps the hoard of 3786 silver coins found by Tsountas had formed the remains of his war chest. Another smaller group of coins seems to have been buried outside the walls at about the same date (**colour plates 23 & 24**) though Dengate suggests that the occasion for the smaller hoard might have been the earlier invasion by Pyrrhus in 272 BC. A shield, a trophy from this event, was found dedicated in the Sanctuary of Enalyios on the road to the north. Mycenae was on the frontier between Argos and the Corinthians/Achaians to the north and it is doubtless for this reason that Argos was interested in the site of Mycenae and had taken such trouble to repair the fortifications which they themselves had disabled two centuries earlier. The site was also involved in the complex politics which surrounded the campaign of Flaminius against Philip V of Macedon between 198 and 193 BC and the control of the Argolid by the Spartans under the tyrant Nabis. One of the inscriptions from the site deals specifically with this period. This was found reused in a set of rooms just to the south below the end of the Great Ramp.

The reuse of this inscription allows us to give rough dates to the two main phases of Hellenistic occupation. The architecture of the early phase, which doubtless underwent several rebuildings itself, was largely removed in the final phase which must have started in the first quarter of the second century BC. It is from this period that we have the well-documented remains of the Citadel House Area. The pottery evidence indicates that the settlement petered out in the latter part of the century, possibly in the wake of the destruction of Corinth in 146 BC, but the coins suggest a slightly different scenario. Mycenae did not mint coins herself, not even the small bronzes that some other Argive dependencies produced. Her main coinage for everyday use was that of Argos herself and the greatest number of the coins found in Rooms F and G of the Citadel House Area belong to a single type. Dengate suggests that this may indicate either a high point of prosperity when this type was in circulation or that some disaster happened, possibly an earthquake or a sack, because of which many more coins than usual were lost and not recovered. In any case there is neither pottery nor coins which can be dated later than the second half of the second century BC.

Given the flourishing small Hellenistic settlement at Mycenae it is rather surprising that the authors of the first century BC claim that the site was by then quite uninhabited. It has however been pointed out that this may mean only that she was by then quite powerless and indeed by the time of the writers in the Greek Anthology (second century AD) Mycenae had become a byword for lost greatness.

In the *Roman period*, we have a further literary testimony to the site. The traveller Pausanias of the second century AD gives a vivid description of what he was shown which can be interpreted quite readily in the light of what we know of the remains. It is clear that at this point there was sufficient visible for him to be guided over the site. The walls, though they were partially covered, never disappeared from view and the Lion Gate is specifically mentioned. The areas of the various graves would seem to be the areas of the Grave Circles and the Prehistoric Cemetery, probably not actually visible but of which a strong local tradition remained. We cannot suggest what he was shown *within* the walls as the Tomb of Agamemnon. The treasuries he mentions must be the tholos tombs several of which remained partially visible. It has been suggested that they became known as treasuries because of the wealth found within them by looters. Looting may have occurred during the Hellenistic period, as we know that Alexander allowed his troops to plunder the Macedonian royal graves.

From this period too we have some scraps of archaeological evidence: a grave stele and some cist graves from the Kalkani hill, a coin of Julia Domna from the Citadel House Area, a Roman lamp from the Pezoulia slope. It is unlikely that there was significant settlement yet there were at least those to guide Pausanias and his like. But Pausanias is the last to describe the site for a millennium and a half.

12 The site museum

See chapter 8 for an account of the distribution of finds between Athens and the site museum.
All the objects in the figures and plates which have MM (Mycenae Museum) numbers are likely to be on display.

The long-awaited site museum is built and the displays are under preparation. I thank Dr Elisabet Spathari and her assistants for telling me of their plans. This brief account is not, however, intended as a guide, merely an indication of what the visitor may expect; changes will undoubtedly be made during ongoing work before the museum opens to the public.

The building lies to the north down the slope from the Lion Gate beside the Lion Tomb. Several interesting structures were discovered on the site during excavation prior to construction and one area of these has been left open to view beside the building to the west.

In the entrance hall framed by the picture window at the far side there is a model from which the visitor will gain a good idea of the site as a whole. An appreciation of the environment similar in many ways to that in antiquity can be gained from the view. Several chamber tomb cemeteries and the routes of two of the roads leading north can also be seen. The first gallery on the right of the entrance focuses on the Palatial period, on the acropolis of Mycenae and on the settlement around it. The displays start with the Palace itself. It is hoped to include a model suggesting its original appearance as the paucity of artifacts is striking though hardly surprising in view of the denuded nature of the site itself (**20**). The best of the wall paintings are of course in Athens though not all on display there.

At the far end of the room on the left are objects from the houses and workshops outside the walls including both the large collections of pottery from Petsas' House and the House of the Wine Merchant as well as some of the exotica from the warehouse in the House of Shields (again the best of this material is in Athens).

Opposite can be seen the exhibits from the Cult Centre particularly the fresco itself from the Room with the Fresco with the altar in front of it and the objects from here displayed as they were found. It should be remember that this is the largest fresco yet found in situ on the wall of any Mycenaean building. In addition the two important ivories (**colour plates 13 & 14**) were associated with this altar. Among the small items note the hilt plates for the Naue sword (cf **51**), the 'beehive' glass beads (**colour plate 18**) and the group of dedications found together is a small pot (**40**). The large figures of human beings (**37 & 38**) and of snakes (**39**) are still completely unique 30 years after their discovery.

From the far end of the first room the visitor goes down to a gallery where the objects from the cemeteries of the Mycenaean period are displayed. These range from Grave Circle B (**6**) and the more ordinary sections of the Prehistoric Cemetery to the numerous chamber tomb cemeteries which surround the site (**10**). It must be remembered that the elite objects, especially those from Grave Circle A (cf **colour plates 7–9**) are in Athens.

In the small gallery beyond are objects from the Post Mycenaean period. Particularly notable are the shield and helmet from the Sanctuary of Enalyios (**68**) and the krater showing a horse from beside the enclosure wall of the Treasury of Atreus (**69**).

The north section of this gallery is devoted to a display of the highlights of Mycenaean civilisation in the Palatial period: the administration, the Linear B script, trade, religion, artistic accomplishment and daily life, described in chapters 8 & 9.

Glossary

For pottery shapes see **13**, **28**, **54**
For definitions of tomb types see:

tholos tomb	41
chamber tomb	44, 69
shaft grave	31

anastylosis	the Greek word for reconstruction
anta	pilaster or attached column on either side of a doorway
apsidal	with one curved end
carination	'keel-like' used to describe a sharp articulation on pottery
cavea	seating area of theatre
conulus	small conical artifact with central vertical piercing (**42**)
corbel vault	system of roofing with each layer projecting slightly further than the last (**11**)
corvée	feudal system of obligated labour
Daedalic	style of sculpture in the Archaic period, seventh century BC
debitage	small waste material from manufacture
faience	in the Aegean and Egypt used for a soft paste covered with glass like glaze
koma	small fortified settlement or village
larnax	clay bathtub or coffin
megaron	rectangular building with central hearth (often surrounded by four columns) entered from a porch (and often an anteroom); basic house type with these features
orthostat	vertical stone slab
peripteral	with columns on all four sides
pisé	rammed earth or clay for walls
Plesia clay	clay of excellent quality found near Plesia south of Mycenae and much used as mortar and for waterproofing
poros	a soft limestone
propylon	built gateway
rhyton	vessel, probably ritual, with wide rim and hole at lower end: both tall conical and imitating an ostrich egg in shape
sekos	inner shrine
socle	stone foundation for a wall
steatite	soft stone of various colours found both in Crete and in the Argolid
stele	upright stone slab used over a grave
stoa	portico or covered colonnade

Bibliography

Mycenae itself

Schliemann, H. 1878 *Mycenae* London & New York

Including copious references to earlier primary publications:

French, E.B. ed. 1979 *Excavations at Mycenae 1939-1955* British School at Athens Supplementary Volume #12
French, E.B. & Iakovides, S. forthcoming *The Mycenae Atlas*, The Archaeological Society of Athens
Iakovides, S. 1983 *Late Helladic Citadels* Leiden
Mylonas, G.E. 1966 *Mycenae and the Mycenaean Age* Princeton
Mylonas, G.E. 1983 *Mycenae Rich in Gold* Athens
Wace, A.J.B. 1949 *Mycenae, An Archaeological History and Guide* Princeton

The Mycenaean World

General and for Bibliography
Dickinson, O.T.P.K. 1994 *The Aegean Bronze Age* Cambridge
French, E.B. & Wardle, K.A. 1988 *Problems in Greek Prehistory* Bristol
Hooker, J.T. 1976 *Mycenaean Greece* London [Bibliography updated to 1981: *Liverpool Classical Monthly* 6.4, 97-111]
Treuil, R. *et al.* 1989 *Les Civilisations Égéennes* Paris
Tsountas, Ch. & Manatt, J.I. 1897 *The Mycenaean Age* Athens
Wardle, K.A. & D. 1997 *The Mycenaean World* Bristol

Specific subjects
Antonaccio, C.M. 1995 *An Archaeology of Ancestors* Lanham MD (Post Mycenaean Cult but see Shelton's paper from the 2000 'Lighten our Darkness' conference for the latest ideas)
Bass, G.F. 1987 'Splendours of the Bronze Age' *National Geographic* 172:6 (Ulu Burun Wreck)
Cavanagh, W. & Mee, C. 1998 *A Private Place: Death in Prehistoric Greece* Jonsered
Chadwick, J. 1976 *The Mycenaean World* Cambridge (Textual Evidence)
Cline, E. 1994 *Sailing the Wine Dark Sea* BAR International Series (Near Eastern contacts)
Driessen, J. 'Homère et les tablettes en linéaire B. Mise au point' *L'Antiquité Classique* 61, 1992, 5-37 (Textual Evidence)

Hiesel, G. 1990 *Späthelladische Hausarchitektur* Mainz

Klein, N.L. 1997 'Excavation of the Greek Temples at Mycenae by the British School at Athens' *BSA* 92, 247-322

Küpper, M. 1996 *Mykenische Architektur* Espelkamp

Loader, N.C. 1998 *Building in Cyclopean Masonry* Jonsered

Maran, J. 2001 'Political and Religious Aspects of Architectural Change on the Upper Citadel of Tiryns. The Case of Building T' 113-21 in *Potnia* Aegaeum 22, Liège

Tzedakis, I. & Martlew, H. 1999 *Minoans and Mycenaeans: Flavours of their Time* Athens (Agricultural Produce; Food and Drink) refered to as 'The Minoan-Mycenaean Food Project'

Illustrations

Demakopoulou, K. ed. 1988 *The Mycenaean World: Five Centuries of Early Greek Culture* Athens (Artifacts)

Theocharis, D. 1973 *Neolithic Greece* Athens (The Environment and Traditional Agriculture)

Specialist

In the text various works are cited in abbreviated form for recent specific information or controversial evidence. Those not self explanatory are listed below.

Burns, B. 2000 *Import Consumption in the Bronze Age Argolid (Greece): Effects of Mediterranean Trade on Mycenaean Society* PhD University of Michigan

Dietz, S. 1991 *The Argolid at the Transition to the Mycenaean Age* Copenhagen

Hall, J.M. 1995 'How Argive was the 'Argive Heraion'? The Political and Cultic Geography of the Argive Plain, 900-400 BC' *AJA* 99, 577-613

Kilian-Dirlmeier, I. 1986 'Beobachtungen zu den Schachtgräber von Mykenai und zu den schmuckbeigaben mykenischer Mannergräber' *JRGZM* 33, 159-98

Knauss, J. 1996 'Die Brücke von Mykene, Talübergang oder Talsperre?' 1-70 in *Argolische Studien: alte Strassen – alte Wasserbauten: Wasserbau und Wasserwirtschaft* 77 Munich

Knauss, J 1997 '<<Agamemnoneion phrear>> Der Stausee der Mykener' *AntW* 28.5 381-95
[Both of these ignore the features that would have been covered by the area of water and require the re-dating of the terrace wall of the Shrine by the Bridge (the 'Agamemnoneion') to the Mycenaean period.]

Mountjoy, P.A. 1996 'Asine Chamber Tomb I:1:The Pottery' in Hägg, R *Asine III: Supplementary Studies on the Swedish Excavations 1922-1930* Stockholm

Musgrave, J.H., Neave, R.A.H. and Prag, J. 1995 'Seven Faces from Grave Circle B at Mycenae' *BSA* 90, 107-36

Peltenberg, E. 1991 'Greeting Gifts and Luxury Faience: a Context for Orientalising Trends in Late Mycenaean Greece' 162-79 in Gale, N. ed. *Bronze Age Trade in the Mediterranean*, Jonsered [though presenting an important analysis of the faience objects from the House of Shields gives an assessment of the quality of Palatial craftsmanship now largely abandoned.

Index